KFC
in China

Secret Recipe for Success

KFC in China

Secret Recipe for Success

WARREN K. LIU

JOHN WILEY & SONS (ASIA) PTE LTD

Other Wiley Editorial Offices
John Wiley & Sons, Inc., 111 River Street, Hoboken, NJ 07030, USA
John Wiley & Sons Ltd, The Atrium, Southern Gate,
    Chichester PO19 BSQ, England
John Wiley & Sons (Canada) Ltd, 5353 Dundas Street West,
    Suite 400, Toronto, Ontario M9B 6H8, Canada
John Wiley & Sons Australia Ltd, 42 McDougall Street,
    Milton, Queensland 4064, Australia
Wiley-VCH, Boschstrasse 12, D-69469 Weinheim, Germany

Library of Congress Cataloging-in-Publication Data:
978-0-470-82384-2

Typeset by Alicia Beebe
Printed in Singapore by Saik Wah Press Pte Ltd.
10 9 8 7 6 5 4 3 2

*This book is dedicated to my wife Ingrid, with whom
I have been deeply in love since my early teens and
happily married for over thirty years; and our four
grown children – Mike, Amy, Alex & Bernard – all
of whom have contributed to a fulfilling life.*

*Royalties from the sale of this book will be
donated to institutions whose mission is to
assist needy children and youths in China with
the continuing pursuit of their education.*

CONTENTS

ACKNOWLEDGMENTS

I wish to acknowledge, and thank, the following individuals for their contribution to this book: Edward Tse and Ronald Haddock of Booz Allen Hamilton for permission to use many of the charts adopted in this book; Jerry Liu Ning of Shanghai Tongji IMBA class of 2007 for work related to charting and pagination; my wife Ingrid, and my sons Alex and Bernard for editing the original English manuscript.

Credit is also due to CJ Hwu of John Wiley & Sons (Asia) and Paul French of Access Asia, without whose persistence and dedication the publication of this book would have been impossible.

Special thanks go to Sam Su, president of YUM! Brands China, who pointed out to me factual errors contained in the original English manuscript. Regardless, all materials, ideas, and opinions expressed in this book are entirely the author's, and do not represent in any way or form those of YUM! Brands, or any employee thereof.

PROLOGUE

On November 12, 1987, KFC opened its first restaurant in China a short walking distance from Tiananmen Square. Nearly nine years later, in June 1996, KFC opened its 100th restaurant in China, also in Beijing. In the subsequent nine years between 1996 and 2005, KFC opened 1,400 more restaurants throughout China, fourteen times the number in the previous nine years. What caused such a difference in the magnitude of growth in new restaurant openings between the first and the second nine years?

Nowhere else outside of the U.S. has KFC experienced such rapid growth, an average of 50 percent compound annual growth rate for eighteen straight years. How did KFC China do it? What are the key factors behind its success?

KFC, Pizza Hut, Taco Bell, Long John Silver's, and A&W are all brands under the umbrella of YUM! Brands, Inc., which was spun off from PepsiCo, Inc. in 1997. At the end of 1986, China was not even on KFC's map. By the end of 2005, less than 20 years later, China accounted for 16 percent of YUM! Brands, Inc.'s worldwide corporate earnings, and 14 percent of worldwide revenue. In the next few decades these ratios are expected to grow steadily. What factors caused the impressive growth of revenue and profits? What accounted for the speed of this growth?

At the end of 2005, China's restaurant service industry generated total revenue of RMB880 billion. At the then-prevalent exchange rate, this was slightly over US$100 billion. KFC accounted for 1 percent of the industry total, making it the single largest chain restaurant enterprise in China. How did an American fast-food chain rise to become number one in a country known for, among other things, its culinary sophistication?

Elsewhere around the world KFC lags behind McDonald's in brand equity, market share, and consumer preference. Not in China. Take size, for instance. McDonald's had over 30,000 restaurants around the world at the end of 2005, outnumbering KFC by more than two to one. In China, it's the reverse – KFC outnumbers McDonald's by more than two to one. What explains this anomaly?

These questions have intrigued me for years. In October 1997, I joined Tricon – the predecessor of YUM! Brands – as vice president of Greater China with responsibilities covering supply chain management, restaurant expansion and development, new product development, quality assurance (QA), and information technology (IT). Reporting to Sam Su, president of YUM! Brands Greater China, which included China, Hong Kong, and Taiwan, I was a founding member of the company's Greater China Executive Committee and the Real Estate Committee. Near the end of 2000, I resigned to pursue another career opportunity. Since then, I have had more time to reflect on those three-plus years I spent building a successful operation with a great many very talented and dedicated colleagues at YUM! Brands Greater China.

This book is written with them in mind, for the benefit of those readers who may find themselves fascinated by the amazing success of KFC in China, the outcome of an unlikely combination of being in the right place, at the right time, with the right people – as the Chinese proverb goes, "Tian-Shi, Di-Li, Ren-Ho" – plus a few other factors, including luck.

This book is intended to examine the major contributing factors that catapulted KFC to the top of the Chinese restaurant service industry in less than two decades. It is written with a focus on KFC China's competitive differentiators, and how they jelled in support of a coherent business strategy, and of each other. The successful execution of KFC China's business strategy has since been rewarded with an unlikely industry leadership position in growth, profitability, market share, and brand recognition in one of the world's fastest-growing economies.

KFC – A PIONEER IN CHINA

FROM ONE TO ONE THOUSAND

In Beijing on January 15th, 2004, KFC opened its 1,000th restaurant in China, only a few miles from its very first restaurant in China, which opened near Beijing's Tiananmen Square in November 1987. From one to one thousand restaurants in a little over 16 years is an enviable record. In fact, in the history of KFC, China has the best record of restaurant growth outside its home market of America. No other restaurant company, Chinese or foreign, has achieved such remarkable growth in China to date.

Today KFC is the largest restaurant chain in China, foreign or local, in terms of revenues, profits, and number of outlets. This statement takes into account all restaurant types, not just quick service (QSR), or "fast food," restaurants. What makes this achievement even more amazing is that this leadership position has been achieved, of all the markets around the world, in the People's Republic of China – with a long history of culinary art known for its flavor, variety, and popularity. Few could have imagined KFC's success back in 1987 with the opening of its first restaurant in China.

And the success doesn't stop there. At the end of 2005, nearly 1,500 KFC restaurants could be found in over 350 cities in every province and special administrative region of China except Tibet, outnumbering its archrival, McDonald's, by a margin of two to one. On average, during 2005 each of these 1,500 restaurants generated US$1 million in revenue and a profit margin of approximately 20 percent.

These impressive numbers came during a challenging year that began with the Sudan 1 red-dye incident, which resulted in a public backlash following media reports that some KFC products contained a harmful ingredient, Sudan 1 red dye, and ended with public concerns across the country over avian flu, a bird flu virus that caused dozens of reported deaths in Asia, most of which were blamed on direct and indirect contact with infected poultry. As a result, both average revenue and profit margin per restaurant suffered a decline of up to 20 percent compared to the previous year.

Despite these setbacks in 2005, KFC maintained its strong leadership position within the Chinese restaurant industry, outpaced the industry growth rate, and widened the gap against archrival McDonald's. KFC's corporate parent welcomed its Chinese subsidiary's strong revenue performance and healthy profit margin, both of which have been on a steady rise as a percentage contribution to the corporate total in recent years. To recognize both the past success and future prospect of its China operation, YUM! Brands announced that, effective 2005, the China division would report directly to the corporate office, along with its U.S. division and international division.

Since then, growth has continued unabated. In the fourth quarter of 2007, KFC China celebrated its twentieth anniversary by opening its 2,000th restaurant. Meanwhile, the China division's revenue contribution to YUM! Brands has risen from 14 percent in 2005 to 17 percent in 2006, and 21 percent in 2007. Earnings contribution by the China division has been even more impressive, from 16 percent in 2005 to 20 percent in 2006, and 23 percent in 2007.

If Colonel Sanders, KFC's iconic founder, were alive today, he would probably be amazed by the popularity of his all-American symbol in one of the world's oldest cultures. If opposites do, in fact, attract, then KFC's spectacular success in China must be a match made in heaven. Contrasts abound, in symbols and substance.

The U.S., with 232 years of history, is one of the youngest nations in the developed world. China, on the other hand, enjoys nearly 5,000 years of recorded history. Capitalism versus a mixed economic system or, in the official Chinese government jargon, "socialist market economy." Individualism versus collectivism. Free-market entrepre-neurialism versus state control and public ownership. Expensive technology-intensive automation versus low-cost manual labor. Fast, simple food versus labor-intensive, sophisticated food. An endless list of contrasts can be reeled off.

What factors caused this quintessential American brand to reach such heights in a land so proud of its own culinary tradition, and so full of contradictions in its views towards the West, led by the U.S.?

Among many others, timing was one.

HISTORICAL CONTEXT

Throughout China's history, the idea of a "Middle Kingdom" or "Center of the Universe" has long dominated Chinese self-perception. It reflects a simplified, self-centered, often self-enclosed, classic Chinese view of China, and the world beyond. With the Opium War in 1840 came the collapse of China's self-imposed isolation, followed by this self-centered view of the world. In its place, an ongoing conflict emerged between modern, Western values and the essence of Chinese culture – rooted in feudalism, more often a mixture of Confucianism, Buddhism, Taoism, and other philosophical schools dating back two and a half millennia.

Between the First Opium War in 1840 and the establishment of the Chinese Republic led by Dr. Sun Yat-Sen and his Nationalist Party in 1912, China was deeply embroiled in a conflict between traditional Chinese values and modern, Western values. Under the National-ist Party, which came to be dominated by Chiang Kai-Shek after Dr. Sun's death in 1925, China gradually shifted towards Western ways until the Chinese Communist Party (CCP) came to power in 1949. With Mao Tse-Dong holding a tight grip on power over the next 27 years until his death, China moved further and further away from the West. Between 1949 and the start of China's economic reforms in 1978, China's economy suffered in stagnation as the CCP led the country on a relentless march towards a socialist utopia.

For over a century prior to the Communist revolution, the Chinese economy suffocated under strong Western and Japanese colonial impacts, culminating in the full-scale invasion of China by the

Japanese Imperial Army in 1937. Deeply humiliated and shaken by repeated military defeats and escalating colonial concessions, China was thrown into an on-again, off-again internal struggle between its deeply rooted traditional values and modern, Western values. This philosophical, psychological, and emotional struggle went into a 30-year hibernation after the CCP came to power in 1949. During the Cultural Revolution, which lasted from 1966 to 1976, both traditional Chinese – especially Confucian – and Western values and practices were obliterated.

China's Opening to the World

Officially, China's economic reforms, which were the driving force behind China's modern-day economic revival, began in 1978. In truth, major shifts in China's economic policies, and the resulting transformation in business, cultural, and social values and practices did not take a giant step forward until 1992, when Deng Xiao-Ping made his now-famous journey – his *nanxun* – to southern China, advocating more economic experimentation and greater risk-taking.

During his journey to the south of China, Deng made a revolutionary comment by advocating "Let some get rich first!" In a political environment that placed heavy emphasis on economic equality among all citizens, this was indeed a revolutionary turning point for China's economic reforms. Some did, in fact, heed Deng's advice. In the small farming and fishing village of Shenzhen, some people took his message to heart, transforming the area's economic landscape forever. Today, Shenzhen is a throbbing metropolis in southern China, a living symbol and testimony to the forces of change brought on by China's economic reforms.

Led by Shenzhen, eye-popping transformations unprecedented in human history have since taken place in different provinces, cities, counties, and even rural villages throughout China. Thus was born the largest economic miracle in human history.

With GDP growth averaging well over 9 percent per year since 1978 and foreign currency reserves well above US$1 trillion at the end of 2007 (and climbing), China has delivered a rising standard of living for the vast majority of its citizens since the beginning of the economic reforms. As the move toward a free market accelerated, old problems that had been removed during Mao's era such as rampant corruption, unemployment, inflation, and the uneven distribution of wealth have returned with a vengeance.

KFC's First Opening Near Tiananmen Square

In many ways, the timing of KFC's first restaurant opening in China in 1987 was perfect. It was nine years after the official launch of China's economic reforms, five years ahead of Deng's historic journey to southern China, and three years ahead of McDonald's entry. China had recently been reopened to the West after decades of hiding behind its self-imposed "bamboo curtain." China's citizens, after being cut off from much of the world for decades, now looked to the West – and anything with a Western flavor – with a mixture of curiosity, anxiety, and anticipation.

The location of KFC's first restaurant, within walking distance from the southern edge of Tiananmen Square in Beijing, was an excellent choice. Beijing was the political center of China, and Tiananmen Square was in the center of Beijing. Back in those days, as a Chinese political slogan used to say, "Zheng-Zhi-Gua-Shuai," or "politics reigns supreme!"

While some thought at the time that Shanghai or Guangzhou would make a better choice, in reality it made better business sense for KFC to locate the first restaurant in China's political center at a time when politics still reigned supreme. For the Beijing government's leadership, it required strong political courage to permit such a well-known symbol of American capitalism, considered the worst possible Western enemy not so long ago, to rise and stand so close to the political heart of the country.

On November 12, 1987, the first KFC restaurant opened to the warmest embrace imaginable by the citizens of Beijing and many out-of-town visitors. It was as if decades of hidden curiosity and conflicting emotions toward the West had been unleashed all at once.

Along with fried chicken, there were many other reasons why eager customers queued up outside the door during the first few weeks after the grand opening. Customers were attracted to KFC's Chinese brand name; its American roots; its likeable, grayish, beard-bearing brand spokesperson – Colonel Sanders; the unique restaurant décor; the new way of ordering food; the bright red and blue colors of the brand logo; the American music broadcasted inside the restaurant; and, as an added bonus, a very clean toilet!

Certainly, price was not one of the attractive features. Most Beijing citizens could not afford the relatively high cost of eating out at KFC in those days, as was the case in every other city and village throughout China. From the beginning, eating out at KFC was an expensive but curious, exciting, unique, and brand-new experience never before encountered by a Chinese customer. Although the food was prepared fast, the dining experience itself marked an occasion, a very special event that required savoring with a measured pace. From the beginning, KFC was never a "fast food" experience for the average Chinese consumer. Instead, it was more of a sit-down dining experience. Moreover, dining at a KFC restaurant was like taking a brief tour of America, with all its connotations: political, cultural, time, and space – real or imaginary.

Clearly, the perception of KFC by Chinese consumers during KFC's early years was heavily influenced by China's context at the time, which carried broad and significant implications for KFC's expansion later on. This is especially the case with regard to customer segment targeting and brand positioning, topics to be covered in Chapter 5 of this book.

Behind the Illusion of Size

With more than 1.3 billion people, or one-fifth of the world's total population, China is a dream market for consumer goods companies around the world, from beer to soft drinks, cosmetics to pharmaceuticals, and donuts to burgers. However, among the early entrants, their business results to date have been mixed. Take YUM! Brands, for example: as of early 2008, of four of its brands that have entered China, KFC and Pizza Hut have performed very well, while A&W and Taco Bell have not. Many companies have leapt into China with high hopes, only to beat a quiet retreat later on. Why?

In addition to a variety of uncertainties that normally surround entry into a new country market, one factor that makes entry into China an even more difficult challenge is the complexity of China's population, geography, history, and recent economic development. China is not only the world's most populous nation, it also possesses a massive land area – roughly the size of the U.S. To complicate matters further, China's population density, economic development, and wealth distribution vary greatly from east to west, and from south to north.

As Exhibit 1 illustrates, China's population density is highly uneven. If one drew a straight line between the northernmost point in Heilongjiang Province and the westernmost point of Yunnan Province, approximately 80 percent of China's total population and 40 percent of the total landmass would be found on the eastern side of this artificial dividing line. In other words, 20 percent of China's population lives on 60 percent of China's land west of this artificial line.

Exhibit 1: 2005 Population Distribution in China

Source: Booz Allen Hamilton

Officially, "West" is defined to include twelve provinces and equivalent administrative units including Chongqing, Sichuan, Yunnan, Guizhou, Shaanxi, Gansu, Qinghai, Ningxia, Xinjiang, Guangxi, Inner Mongolia, and Tibet. Together, they account for 71 percent of China's total landmass, and 29 percent of the total population.

While vast areas in western China are sparsely populated, China's eastern seacoast is among the world's most densely populated. Up until the turn of the last century, economic development and wealth accumulation were largely confined to China's eastern seacoast, especially in southeastern China, where 20 percent of the country's population generated half of the nation's GDP and three-quarters of its total exports at one point in time.

Aside from population density, economic contrasts between China's eastern and western regions are staggering. Per capita gross domestic product (GDP) in the West is 58 percent of the national average, far below that of the East. For example, the per capita GDP of Chongqing, the most populous city in the West and the nation's capital during the Japanese invasion of China from the late 1930s through the mid 1940s, is merely one-fifth that of Shanghai. Both belong to an elite group of only four cities (known as municipalities) in China that report directly to the central government (the other two are Beijing and Tianjin). As Exhibit 2 shows, the average disposable income between eastern and western China follows a similar pattern.

Exhibit 2: 2005 Average Disposable Income Distribution in China

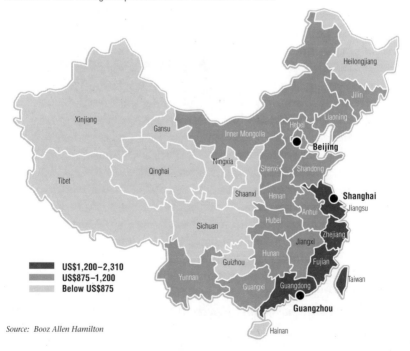

US$1,200–2,310
US$875–1,200
Below US$875

Source: Booz Allen Hamilton

URBAN TRANSFORMATION

Both the scope and the speed of change during the last 20 years in almost all of China's urban centers have been mind-boggling. Before 1990, for example, the Lujiazui area in Shanghai's Pudong District was a collection of rice paddies and low-lying huts. Today it is a thriving banking community with dozens of skyscrapers, one of which houses the world's tallest hotel, the Jinmao Grand Hyatt. From the hotel lobby located on the 54th floor, visitors from around the world gather to catch a glimpse of the Shanghai skyline and the world-famous Bund across the Huangpu River.

While the skylines of Shenzhen, Shanghai, and Beijing have long symbolized China's economic transformation, many of the second-tier cities around the country such as Shenyang, Qingdao, and Xian had already begun the process of face-lifting by the turn of the century. More recently, even third and fourth-tier cities – some such as Urumqi and Lhasa, which are located in western China – have begun major face-lifting transformations. The magnitude, pervasiveness, and speed of these transformations can be mind-boggling.

Take Qingdao, home of the famous beer brand by the same name (Tsingtao), for example. In 2000, my colleagues and I traveled there to inspect existing and proposed restaurant sites. During the brief visit, we learned about a major development project by the city government that would move the city's commercial district from the old downtown to a new area. At the time, the only visible landmarks in this proposed new commercial area included the city hall, a shopping mall, and a five-star hotel – all of which had been recently constructed.

When I returned to Qingdao in early 2004, a brand new city full of skyscrapers had risen over the horizon, overlooking this beautiful coastal retreat known for its German architecture. And Qingdao is not alone. Similar stories could be told for a countless number of cities large and small throughout China.

Shopping Chinese Style

In parallel to massive infrastructure projects undertaken by the Chinese government to build new cities, roads, airports, or, for that matter, the world's fastest commercial rapid-transit system – the magnetic levitation (Maglev) train in Shanghai, with a top speed of 430 kilometers, or 270 miles, per hour – Chinese consumers have made significant changes to their spending and lifestyle patterns since the beginning of China's economic reforms.

China's retail industry provides a good example of the rapid succession of changes that have taken place in recent years. Up until the late 1980s, "shopping" in China was a necessity, not a form of relaxation or enjoyment. Most major consumer purchases took place inside department stores or specialty stores, all of which were state-owned and operated. Product selection was poor. Good customer service was non-existent.

In 1992, China's State Council, the country's highest administrative authority, decided to allow foreign investment in the retail industry. Changes began to take place almost overnight. By the end of 2004, when China was required to fully open its retail sector to foreign investors under the terms of its accession to the World Trade Organization (WTO), China had given the green light to 314 foreign retailers and wholesalers. Bringing a whole new approach to the Chinese retail market, these newcomers from abroad had opened 4,000 retail stores of varying type and size, occupying a total of 9.2 million square meters, in the top few dozen cities in China.

Foreign investment in the retail industry accelerated in 2005. In a single year, China approved another 1,000 foreign retailers and wholesalers, allowing them to open 1,160 stores with an operational area of 4.7 million square meters. Of these new foreign stores, specialized stores representing well-known, high-end brands such as Armani, Hugo Boss, Gucci, and Zegna accounted for 57.2 percent. Hypermarkets made up 25.5 percent, and department stores accounted for 13.1 percent.

Today, millions of Chinese consumers flock to foreign retail stores such as B&Q from the U.K., Carrefour from France, Isetan and Jusco from Japan, Lotus from Thailand, Metro from Germany, Parkson from Malaysia, and Wal-Mart from the U.S. on any given day in a growing number of Chinese cities. Relying on their superior knowledge of the local market, local players like Lianhua and NongGongShang are also fighting for a piece of the action with improved quality of service, upgraded store facilities and back-room systems, and modern management techniques, spurred on by their formidable competitors from overseas and rising consumer expectations.

Compared to the late 1980s, the typical shopping experience for the average urban Chinese consumer has undergone a seismic revolution. In many ways, shoppers in the largest Chinese cities have more choice of international brands today than their counterparts in New York, Paris, or Tokyo. Moreover, while it took decades or even longer for developed economies to evolve their retail distribution channels from mom-and-pop corner shops to department stores, supermarkets, hypermarkets, specialty shops, and convenience stores, the same process of retail evolution took place in China in less than 15 years. Similar fast-paced, often generation-skipping, industry transformations have taken place across the Chinese economy in telecommunications, transportation, electronics, and manufacturing industries. More recently, similar changes have taken place in service industries such as banking, insurance, and even government services. The net effect of these developments across multiple economic sectors is the co-existence of old and new generations of technologies, products, and channels of distribution in almost every single direction one turns, at a speed of change seldom seen anywhere else around the world.

Exhibit 3: Chinese Per Capita GDP, 1995–2005 (US$)

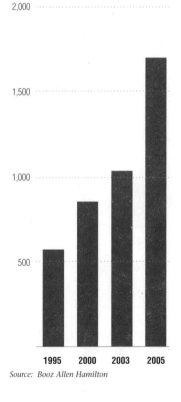

Source: Booz Allen Hamilton

ECONOMIC REFORMS

Since the beginning of China's economic reforms in 1978, China's economic performance has made a dramatic turn for the better. With GDP growing at an average of more than 9 percent per year, China has overtaken Germany to become the world's third-largest economy, behind the U.S. and Japan. In 2003, the country passed another important milestone when per capita GDP exceeded US$1,000 for the first time, as Exhibit 3 illustrates.

Of course, dramatic changes taking place in China during the past 30 years have gone far beyond GDP growth or, for that matter, growth of per capita GDP. Exhibit 4 shows growth in per capita disposable income since 2001, in terms of both market exchange rate and purchasing power parity (PPP).

Exhibit 4: Growth in Per Capita Disposable Income, 2001–2005

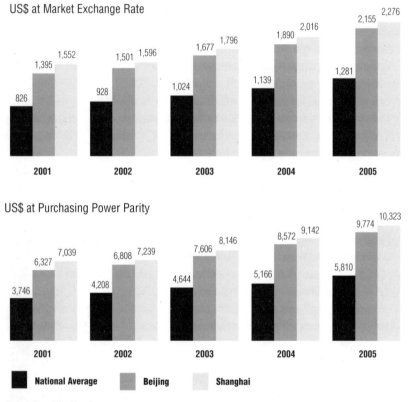

Source: *Booz Allen Hamilton*

While the standard of living for the average Chinese citizen has clearly improved, China's economic reforms have created new economic challenges. These include, among others: corruption;

unemployment; inadequate social welfare system; environmental pollution; waste and inefficiency of resource utilization; uneven distribution of wealth, education, infrastructure, and public health facilities between different geographical regions, and between urban centers and rural villages.

One Nation, Two Economies

A German diplomat who had been stationed in China for years recently observed that China is like a country with two separate economies. The more developed urban centers along the Pacific coast resemble western Europe. The less-developed countryside in the western interior resembles much of Africa. Undoubtedly, there is some exaggeration in this gross oversimplification, but it delivers an important message.

Over the past quarter-century, numerous examples of "China's Africa" could have been observed in places like Sanjiang, Guangxi; Xiangcheng, Sichuan; Yanbi and Yuenyang, Yunnan; Yumen, Gansu; or western Shandong, one of the more affluent provinces in eastern China. Although people living in these and similar places, most of them in rural and western China, have also benefited from China's economic reforms, they have not benefited nearly as much as urban dwellers.

The gap between urban and rural China is huge in terms of both population density and consumer purchasing power. On population density, according to official statistics, China had 668 cities at the beginning of 2004, half of them with populations in excess of 200,000. Thirty-seven of them had a population of over one million, led by Chongqing, with 31 million; Shanghai, 16 million; and Beijing, 14 million. The great majority of these top 37 population centers are in eastern China.

In terms of purchasing power, China's top ten cities account for 20 percent of national retail sales; the top 30 cities – of which only four are located in western China, account for one-third. Furthermore, based on data from 2004, China's urban per capita income of US$1,531 is more than three times the rural per capita income of US$488. These statistics contributed to China's alarmingly high Gini Index, which measures the degree of wealth concentration. Worse yet, income disparity continues to grow at an alarming rate.

On the other hand, up to 200 million rural Chinese have migrated to urban centers over the past two decades in search of job opportunities and a higher standard of living. Thus, while rural Chinese accounted for almost 80 percent of the country's total population in 1978, they account for less than 60 percent today. In the next few decades, as the rural population continues its gradual decline through rising migration into urban centers, the current concerns over the growing urban/rural income gap will be replaced by the increasing disparities between the urban rich and the urban poor.

The worsening economic gap between rural and urban China has finally caught the attention of the Chinese government. At the National People's Congress (NPC) convened in March 2006, Chinese Premier Wen Jia-Bao announced a new program initiative entitled "The New Socialist Countryside." This program is designed to spur the economic development and raise the standard of living in rural China through infrastructure projects to improve roads, electricity, water, education, and health care.

In addition to the changes mentioned above, the entire economic structure in China has undergone major transformations. In 1978, all

Exhibit 5: China Food Service Industry Size and Growth (US$bn)

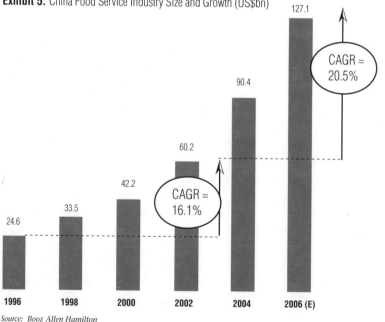

Source: *Booz Allen Hamilton*

of China's business enterprises were owned and operated by the state. Today, only about 30–40 percent are state-owned enterprises (SOEs). In the past few years, many of the remaining bastions of state ownership, including banking, insurance, brokerage, and other segments of the financial services sector, have opened up to foreign investment.

CHINA'S RESTAURANT INDUSTRY

Reflecting the growth of the overall economy and rising consumer prosperity, China's restaurant industry closed 2005 with total revenue reaching RMB880 billion, or slightly over US$100 billion based on the then-prevalent exchange rate. For the industry as a whole, this represented yet another year of double-digit growth. KFC accounted for approximately 1 percent of this industry total, making it the clear leader in terms of both revenue and profit in a highly fragmented industry.

As can be seen from Exhibits 5 and 6, while China's food service industry has been growing at approximately 20 percent per annum, the QSR sector has grown even faster, accounting for 45 percent of the industry total at the end of 2005. By comparison, this is up from 27 percent in 1998. In order to maintain its market share in China, KFC must keep up with the projected industry growth rate of 20 percent or more in the years ahead. That will not be an easy task.

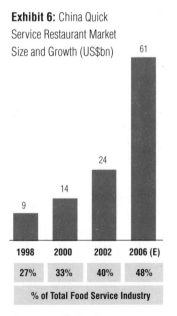

Exhibit 6: China Quick Service Restaurant Market Size and Growth (US$bn)

1998	2000	2002	2006 (E)
9	14	24	61
27%	33%	40%	48%

% of Total Food Service Industry

Source: Booz Allen Hamilton

KFC's Growth Path in China

KFC's growth path in China followed the development of the larger economy, beginning with cities, counties, and townships within provinces along the eastern coast throughout the late 1980s and the mid-1990s. In 1995, upon entering Chengdu, the capital city of Sichuan Province, KFC kicked off its westward expansion. Two years later, the brand's establishment in Chongqing further solidified KFC's market position in western China. At the same time, market entry into Wuhan and Changsha pushed KFC inland to central China. Together, these market entry decisions later proved to be decisions with foresight. In 1999, China's central government officially launched a state-sponsored program to develop China's western region in an attempt to alleviate the growing imbalance between the increasingly affluent eastern coast and the landlocked inland west.

Specifically, KFC China's timetable for new market entry during the first decade looked like this:

1987 – Beijing
1989 – Shanghai
1992 – Nanjing
1993 – Suzhou, Hangzhou, Wuxi, Guangzhou, and Qingdao
1994 – Fuzhou, Tianjin, and Shenyang
1995 – Chengdu, Dalian, and Wuhan
1996 – Shenzhen and Xiamen
1997 – Changsha and Chongqing

The boundaries between these KFC markets are usually drawn along China's administrative units – made up of 22 provinces, five autonomous regions and four "super cities," or municipalities – and combinations thereof. Thus, KFC Nanjing market oversees Jiangsu Province while KFC Chengdu market oversees Sichuan Province, etc.

By the end of the 1990s, almost all of China's top 100 cities listed in Exhibit 7 had been penetrated by KFC. They represent China's largest population centers. Approximately one-third of them are important political centers, either as provincial capitals or equivalent, or as one of four centrally administered "super cities."

Once a new KFC market is established, it is registered as a legal entity with various provincial and local government authorities. Organizationally, a KFC market is structured as a profit and loss center headed by a market general manager, with its own organization, dedicated staff, and annual operating budget. This structure is very similar to KFC China's national headquarters, internally referred to as the Shanghai Restaurant Support Center, as illustrated in Exhibit 8. Prior to 2002, YUM! Brands went by the name of "Tricon."

Over the years, KFC's expansion in China has proven to be well timed. By first entering China in 1987, it was well positioned to take

Exhibit 7: Top 100 Population Centers In China

★ Capital or major cities
● Smaller cities

Top 100 Population Centers List (*not* in the order of population rankings):

North China	Central China	39. Xuzhou	62. Yantai	South China
1. Beijing	19. Wuhan	40. Wenzhou	63. Zibo	82. Guangzhou
2. Tianjing	20. Changsha	41. Changshu	64. Dongying	83. Shenzhen
3. Shijiazhuang	21. Xian	42. Hefei	65. Weifang	84. Zhuhai
4. Taiyuan	22. Taiyuan	43. Xiaoshan	66. Weihai	85. Dongguan
5. Tangshan	23. Zhengzhou	44. Zhangjiagang	67. Rongcheng	86. Foshan
6. Baotou	24. Nanchang	45. Taizhou	68. Jining	87. Haikou
7. Qinghuangdao	25. Luoyang	46. Wujiang	69. Laizhou	88. Shantou
	26. Zhuzhou	47. Nantong	70. Linyi	89. Nanning
Northeast	27. Shiyan	48. Zhenjiang	71. Zhaozhuang	90. Nanhai
8. Dalian	28. Xiangfan	49. Yiwu	72. Xiamen	91. Panyu
9. Changchun		50. Kunshan	73. Fuzhou	92. Shunde
10. Harbin	East China	51. Huzhou	74. Jinjiang	93. Zhanjiang
11. Shenyang	29. Shanghai	52. Cixi	75. Quanzhou	94. Zhongshan
12. Anshan	30. Hangzhou	53. Taichang		95. Liuzhou
13. Daqing	31. Wuxi	54. Yuhang	Southwest	96. Huadu
14. Pangjin	32. Ningbo	55. Yuyao	76. Kunming	97. Xinhui
15. Jilin	33. Nanjing	56. Yancheng	77. Guiyang	
16. Fushun	34. Jiangyin	57. Danyang	78. Yuxi	Northwest
17. Benxi	35. Suzhou	58. Taixing		98. Urumqi
18. Qiqihar	36. Yixing	59. Maanshan	West China	99. Lanzhou
	37. Yangzhou	60. Qingdao	79. Chengdu	100. Karamay
	38. Changzhou	61. Jinan	80. Chongqing	
			81. Panzhihua	

Source: Booz Allen Hamilton

Exhibit 8: Organization Structure of Tricon Shanghai Restaurant Support Center, Circa 1998

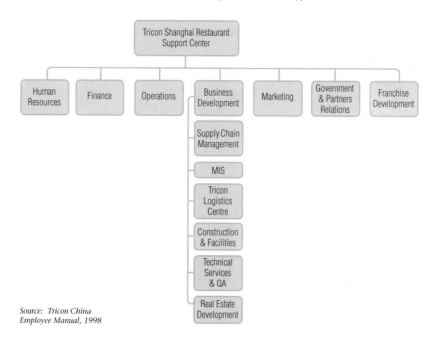

Source: Tricon China
Employee Manual, 1998

full advantage of the acceleration of China's economic reforms, which came five years later. KFC's second big expansion began in 1995 when it expanded into China's western region, four years before the official kick-off of a major government-led program to develop the region's full economic potential. On both occasions, KFC demonstrated an ability to anticipate emerging market forces and government policies, a unique skill set that is critical to the success of any company doing business in China's "socialist market economy."

KFC in Asia

Although many consumers around the world know that KFC was the brainchild of Colonel Sanders, few are aware of the company's turbulent history in Asia, especially within Greater China, which includes Mainland China, Hong Kong, Macau, and Taiwan.

During the 1930s, when he was in his late forties, Colonel Sanders invented a special method of deep-frying chicken based on a recipe consisting of eleven different ingredients. Thus was born the world-famous Original Recipe Kentucky Fried Chicken. In 1952, Colonel Sanders began the development of the KFC franchise. By 1957, KFC had expanded to 400 restaurants through franchise. When Colonel Sanders sold his franchise in 1964 for US$2 million, KFC had over 600 restaurants across North America.

Over the years, the ownership of KFC changed a few times. In 1971, Heublein, an American spirits and food distributor, purchased KFC for US$275 million. In 1982, R.J. Reynolds Industries acquired Heublein and KFC became its subsidiary. In 1986, PepsiCo Inc. acquired KFC for US$840 million from R.J. Reynolds. Eleven years later, in 1997, PepsiCo divested its restaurant group in order to focus on two other product groups: soda and snacks. At that time, three restaurant brands made up PepsiCo's restaurant group: KFC, Pizza Hut, and Taco Bell. With the divestiture, Tricon was born.

In the ensuing years, Tricon acquired additional restaurant brands including A&W, best known for its classic root beer; and Long John Silver's, a brand known for its seafood selections. These additions required a name change to YUM! Brands in 2002.

KFC's foray into Asia began with Japan in 1970. Within Greater China, KFC first entered Hong Kong in 1973 and quickly grew to eleven restaurants in the following year. But KFC misjudged the local market and failed to develop a suitable business model. All eleven restaurants were closed in early 1975. Ten years later, KFC returned to Hong Kong and persevered this time, eventually franchising its operation to a company called Birdland, which was backed by a group of local investors.

In 1984, KFC entered Taiwan through a franchise agreement with a joint venture company set up by two large Japanese trading companies and a local food company called the Uni-President Group. Later, Birdland took over the KFC franchise in Taiwan from the original joint venture company.

In 1996, the YUM! Brands Greater China headquarters in Shanghai began opening its own KFC restaurants in Taiwan in tandem with Birdland, without an agreement between the two companies to divide up the territory. Until 2001, when Birdland sold its franchise back to KFC, there had been a period of five years during which both companies tried, in good faith, to co-manage the KFC brand in Taiwan. During that period, their business relationship was often cooperative, sometimes competitive, and always challenging, given the nature of a franchiser/franchisee relationship.

KFC's rocky experience in Asia, especially its early failures in Hong Kong and Taiwan during the 1970s and the 1980s, served as valuable and relatively inexpensive lessons in preparation for its 1987 entry into China, which later proved to be the most critical country market for KFC in Asia, or anywhere else outside the U.S.

An American Pioneer in China

There is little doubt that KFC was a pioneer when it entered China in 1987, the significance of which goes far beyond the fact that KFC was the first well-known Western restaurant brand to enter China. At the time of its market entry, KFC introduced at least two new concepts to China: fast food and restaurant chains.

Prior to KFC's entry in 1987, some might argue that there were already various forms of Chinese fast food being served. These ranged from the traditional Chinese breakfast items including congee, soy bean milk, and *yiu-tiao* (fritters of twisted dough), to noodles, various other snacks, and even selections of regular Chinese dishes already cooked – some kept warm, while others were served cold as appetizers – such as *bao-zi* (Chinese steamed buns), *jiao-zi* (Chinese water dumplings), sweetened baked goods of various types, and even Cantonese dim sum.

Unlike most Chinese food, which requires elaborate and time-consuming preparation, these Chinese "fast foods" are usually prepared in advance of purchase, or can be prepared relatively quickly upon placement of an order because of their simplicity. Most of the catering units are small in scale, lacking sufficient financial capital, an attractive physical appearance, a group of properly trained employees, and a clean and well-maintained dining, kitchen, and lavatory environment. While the food may be served fast and its price may be affordable, this is usually because of the simplicity of the food offered and the lack of a desirable restaurant environment.

This type of fast food is very different from KFC's concept of fast food. First, KFC food is prepared quickly because of systemization, process standardization, and equipment automation, none of which is evident in the preparation of traditional Chinese "fast food." Second, the physical characteristics of KFC restaurants are very different from the traditional Chinese catering units. They are cleaner, brighter, more relaxed, and require more financial investment. Third, food from KFC restaurants is priced at a significant premium compared to Chinese "fast food." Therefore, it is no exaggeration to conclude that KFC introduced the concept of fast food or, at the very least, a much higher standard of fast food, to China.

Before KFC arrived on the scene, there were very few Chinese restaurant groups that operated multiple restaurant units in different parts of China with the same brand name and under the same ownership. Of those, the number of restaurants in each group was very small, usually a handful, located in the same city or province. In less than a decade, KFC succeeded in developing a multi-province, multi-city chain of restaurants covering an ever-expanding territory and, before long, the whole of China. In doing so, KFC successfully transplanted a proven business model from America to China: a restaurant chain.

Prior to KFC, why were there no Western fast-food restaurants in China, and why was there not any sizeable restaurant chain, local and otherwise? On the first question, the short answer is that China lacked broad economic affluence and an emerging middle class prior to the 1990s, conditions often associated with the rise in popularity of Western fast food. On the second question, the short answer is that Chinese food comes in many different varieties, and Chinese consumers in different parts of the country prefer different styles of Chinese food.

With the wide variety of Chinese dishes, ingredients, and complexity in their preparation, it is not easy to standardize the "production" process for one Chinese dish, let alone dozens or hundreds of them. Without process automation, the idea of product duplication with universal adherence to tight standards and consistently high quality, which is a fundamental precept behind a fast-food restaurant chain, would be virtually impossible.

The first appearance of KFC in China in 1987 brought not only American fast food, but also a major foreign restaurant brand. Even more important, it brought a sweeping revolution with a new approach to food preparation, restaurant operation, and business management to the Chinese restaurant industry, underpinned by the dual concepts of fast food and restaurant chains. Both concepts were new to China.

2

ASSEMBLE AND RETAIN THE MOST QUALIFIED TEAM

INTRODUCTION

Numerous management studies have concluded that one of the key drivers for long-term business success lies in a stable and effective leadership team. KFC in China is no exception. Its current leadership team has been working together for well over a decade, building a high-growth, increasingly profitable business from scratch.

It began with a group of ethnic Chinese expatriates recruited from Taiwan and other countries throughout Asia in the early 1990s. Together, these experienced, energetic, and entrepreneurial restaurant operators went about building a chain of restaurants and the infrastructure to support them rapidly, first on the eastern coast of China and, beginning in the mid-1990s, further into China's western inland. To build and expand, these expatriate Chinese relied on their past industry experience accumulated outside China, combining it with a spirit of innovation and an instinctive knowledge about China – language, history, culture, customs, and values.

Early on, they realized that in order to succeed, they needed thousands, even tens of thousands, of local employees who were just as experienced and skillful with the industry's ways as they were. To achieve this, they had the foresight to build a very practical and effective system that combines employee training with restaurant operation.

Once talents had been recruited and trained, they further recognized the need to motivate and retain these talents through attractive compensation, opportunities for career development and growth, a respectable brand based on industry leadership, and a winning company culture.

THE PIONEERS

Roger was born in Taipei, Taiwan in 1956. He worked hard all his life, first as a student and, later on, as a salary man. Like most of his peers growing up in Taiwan, Roger was used to a highly competitive education system with pressure for academic achievements coming from his parents and teachers at a young age – from the time he was in kindergarten. Later on in life, when Roger attended a four-year technical college majoring in food science, he began working part-time in a McDonald's restaurant in the suburbs of Taipei. That's where Roger met his future wife, Elaine, and some of their closest friends for life. After graduating from college, Roger joined McDonald's full time, and within a few years he was promoted to the position of restaurant manager. Three years later, Roger was promoted to oversee several more restaurants. In between, he married Elaine.

One morning in December 1995, Roger received a telephone call from a headhunter. The headhunter found him through an ex-colleague who is now working for KFC in China. By then, Roger had already heard about KFC's aggressive expansion plan in China through other colleagues and friends in the QSR industry. The QSR industry in Taiwan is a small circle, where people know each other directly or through common acquaintances.

As it turned out, Roger had thought about the prospect of pursuing his career in China even before the headhunter's call. Both McDonald's and KFC had huge expansion plans for China, and both had been aggressively opening new markets and new restaurants in China. A few months earlier, he had expressed a strong interest in exploring future career opportunities in McDonald's China during a private career development session with his immediate superior. To his surprise, KFC contacted him about just such an opportunity first.

It was an important career decision for Roger, one that required close consultation with Elaine, and their parents. Together, Roger and Elaine began to list the pros and cons of staying with McDonald's Taiwan versus joining KFC China.

The list of pros of staying with McDonald's Taiwan included:

1. Staying close to their aging parents, although both Roger and Elaine had brothers and sisters who could look after their parents while they were away in China. Besides, their parents escaped to Taiwan from the Chinese Mainland with the Nationalist Party back in 1949, and supported the idea that Roger and Elaine return to their homeland to live and work.

2. Roger and Elaine's only daughter would begin kindergarten in a year and, soon thereafter, primary education. Staying in Taiwan meant she would be able to receive a good education, one both Roger and Elaine were familiar with.

3. Both Roger and Elaine had been well recognized within McDonald's Taiwan for their outstanding job performance. Both had been targeted for further grooming. Staying with McDonald's Taiwan meant staying close to friends, colleagues, and successful career tracks. In addition, Roger and Elaine wouldn't have to bear the guilt of "betraying" McDonald's by joining a direct competitor.

4. Staying with McDonald's Taiwan meant not having to deal with the uncertainties surrounding a move to China, including a lower standard of living and the rumored inadequate hospital facilities – which was an important consideration since Elaine was pregnant with their second child.

On the other hand, joining KFC China presented certain attractive features:

1. China is a big market, with seemingly unbounded potential for KFC, which had clearly passed the "Chinese taste bud" test in Taiwan, Hong Kong, Singapore, and other markets

around the world where ethnic Chinese were congregated. The future of KFC China was not without risk, but the potential for faster career advancement far outweighed the potential risks.

2. Despite political differences between China and Taiwan, China was the birthplace of Roger and Elaine's parents and their forefathers. Ever since first grade, they had learned in school, and at home, everything they needed in order to fit relatively effortlessly into China – including China's language, history, literature, geography, music, food, and values.

3. KFC China was offering attractive expatriate compensation, relocation, and benefit packages including hardship allowance, housing subsidy, children's education allowance, company-provided automobile, and other benefits.

4. While politically, Taiwan and China seemed at times to be a world apart, geographically China was only a stone's throw away. In the worst case, Roger and Elaine could always decide to return to Taiwan if KFC China did not work out for them.

With these thoughts in mind, Roger and Elaine decided they would continue their dialogue with KFC through the headhunter, as a couple. Four months later, Roger, Elaine, and their daughter Amy landed in Shanghai. As part of their agreement with KFC, Roger and Elaine would be heading up different functions in KFC China's headquarters in Shanghai.

That was 1996. Not too long ago, Roger, Elaine, and their two daughters celebrated their tenth anniversary in Shanghai. Today, both of them remain employed with KFC China, with no regret whatsoever about the decision they jointly made more than a decade ago.

The "Taiwan Gang"

Roger and Elaine's path to China is typical of the senior management team of KFC China throughout the 1990s.

KFC China's leadership team has sometimes been dubbed the "Taiwan Gang." In truth, many were born and raised in Taiwan like Sam

Su, president of YUM! Brands China, Roger, and Elaine, while others came from Hong Kong, Indonesia, Malaysia, Singapore, and even the U.S. All, with few exceptions, are experienced restaurant operators having grown up and been educated in an environment with Chinese as their first language, with instinctive knowledge about Chinese culture and values. Many came from a background with McDonald's. All shared the excitement of leaving a relatively mature QSR market at home in order to pursue a potentially huge new market opportunity in China. The prospect of building an empire from the ground level up, full of uncertainty, excitement, and potential rewards is an experience of a lifetime few of them would willingly forfeit.

During the first decade in China, between 1987 and 1997, KFC did not have a sufficient number of internal candidates to meet its growth-led demand for restaurant managers, area managers who supervise up to six restaurants, district managers who supervise up to four areas, and market general managers who can oversee the profit and loss of a hundred-million-dollar market such as KFC Shanghai or KFC Beijing.

The shortage of trained and experienced restaurant management staff can be traced to the fact that developing an exceptional management trainee to become a district manager takes a minimum of five years. As a result, through the mid-1990s, nearly all KFC market general managers and district managers were recruited from abroad. They were experienced ethnic Chinese QSR operators. By 1997, only one of the 15 KFC market general managers was a local Chinese. In addition, through the 1990s, the heads of all functions in KFC's Greater China headquarters in Shanghai, positions which usually carried the title of senior manager and, more often, director and vice president, were nearly all ethnic Chinese expatriates.

In other words, members of the "Taiwan Gang" dominated the top leadership team of KFC China throughout the 1990s. It is this group of ethnic Chinese entrepreneurs rich in fast-food restaurant operational experience and instinctive knowledge about China that made a huge difference in establishing a strong foundation for KFC in China. At its peak, close to one hundred of them filled the most senior positions in KFC China, both in the field and in the Shanghai headquarters.

Why were there so many ethnic Chinese from Taiwan who dominated the KFC China leadership team? First, the numbers tell the story. That is, with a population of 23 million, which is three to five times that of Hong Kong and Singapore, Taiwan has a natural advantage. The numerical superiority of Taiwan is naturally reflected in the number of Western QSRs found there in comparison to Hong Kong and Singapore. With hundreds of units of Burger King, KFC, McDonald's and other top QSR chains already operating in Taiwan by the early 1990s, Taiwan had a far larger pool of restaurant management talents compared to Hong Kong and Singapore.

Second, generally speaking, those who received their primary and secondary education in Taiwan during the second half of the last century have had a solid grounding in Chinese history, culture, literature, geography, values, and language – both written and spoken – oftentimes even more so compared to their peers born and raised on the Mainland. The same cannot be said about ethnic Chinese from Hong Kong or Singapore, at least not through the twentieth century. My own extensive travels throughout Asia in the 1980s and the first half of the 1990s convinced me that English, Cantonese, and various dialects from China's Fujian Province were far more popular than Mandarin in news media as well as in casual conversations among local ethnic Chinese populations in Hong Kong and Singapore. In fact, it was a rarity to find ethnic Chinese fluent in the Mandarin dialect back in those days in either Hong Kong or Singapore. Since 1949, Mandarin has been the official dialect of China, a country with hundreds of local dialects, many of which are as prohibitive as foreign languages.

More importantly, while the mandatory education system in Taiwan during the second half of the last century under the Nationalist government was very much China-centric in its material contents, such was not the case in Hong Kong and Singapore.

Alternatives to Staffing a Leadership Team

Other foreign companies chose to staff their leadership team in China differently from KFC back in the 1980s and 1990s. Some of them relied on non-Chinese expatriates, usually from a company's home country. Others relied on ethnic Chinese from Hong Kong, Singapore and, to a lesser extent, Indonesia, Malaysia, Thailand, and elsewhere around the world. One direct competitor of KFC, for example, assigned a

Singaporean Chinese during part of the 1990s and through the early 2000s as the head of its China operation based in Hong Kong. Many senior members of its China leadership team were ethnic Chinese from Hong Kong and the U.S., but they were unable to read and write Chinese characters, or converse in Mandarin. No reasonable human being can expect such a leadership team to be able to communicate effectively with the people they lead, or be able to make the most effective and timely decisions in a highly complex and dynamic marketplace such as China.

Of course, Western companies hiring ethnic Chinese managers from Hong Kong or Singapore to lead their China operations are not necessarily wrong in doing so. On average, ethnic Chinese from Singapore and Hong Kong are better at the English language and more in tune with Western ways of thinking compared to their Taiwanese counterparts. Taiwanese Chinese, on the other hand, received a compulsory China-centered education as opposed to a mixed English-Chinese one. As a result, their command of the Chinese language, knowledge about China, and their emotional attachment to China – especially those descendants of Mainland Chinese who retreated with the Nationalist Party to Taiwan around 1949 – tend to be stronger.

Ultimately, the screening criteria for the selection of a leadership team in China depends on the nature of a company's product, target market segments, timing of entry, and a number of other factors. For KFC, as a pioneer in a foreign market with no industry-experienced local talent available, while selling a product closely linked to the core of China's culture, the "Taiwan Gang" was the best choice available at the time.

Today, Western companies face a much broader range of choices when it comes to leadership selection, including local Chinese born and raised in China with years of multinational company work experience, many of them Western-trained – both academically and professionally.

Bottlenecks to Rapid Growth

During the first nine years in China, KFC opened 100 restaurants. In the ensuing nine years KFC opened an additional 1,400. What caused this order-of-magnitude difference in new restaurant openings between two back-to-back nine-year periods? Deliberate strategy? Rocky beginnings? A growth momentum that required time to develop? Time needed to construct and validate a successful operating model? Inadequate cash flow to propel self-funded growth? Resource constraints related to supplies, distribution, and logistics? The answer is, all of the above, and more. Among the causes, the single most critical bottleneck that prevented faster growth in KFC's first nine years in China was the shortage of experienced restaurant management staff, a direct result of the combination of straight-forward arithmetic and restaurant operational requirements.

An average KFC restaurant in China requires five or more managers at four or five levels, depending on restaurant volume. Each restaurant general manager takes two years or more to develop from a management trainee, who is usually a recent college graduate. And the best way to train future restaurant managers is to put them to work in an operating restaurant, not in a "school" or other simulated environment. Therefore, to have enough restaurant management talents to staff new restaurant openings first requires a critical mass of existing restaurants suitable for in-restaurant training. It's a classic "chicken or egg" problem.

Not all restaurants are suitable for operational training. Some are too new, with relatively inexperienced management teams in place. Others are too busy, or not busy enough. When KFC had ten restaurants spread over a big territory, it took a long time to grow the next ten because each one was a new "hub" a long distance away from the next. When the number of restaurants grew to 100 with some clusters, the task of growing the next ten became much easier and took far less time, especially when the next new restaurant was physically close to one of these clusters. Physical proximity is important due to cost and convenience factors. When the total number of operating restaurants grew to a thousand, the task of growing the next ten, even hundred, became as easy as snapping a finger. Well, almost.

Under these circumstances, "double decking" of restaurant management staff in select restaurants in order to train the next wave of new restaurant operation management staff is not only unavoidable, but also necessary at all times.

Fast Development of Local Restaurant Management Talent

Of all the contributions made by members of the "Taiwan Gang," the training and development of local restaurant management teams to keep up with restaurant unit growth over the years is one of the most significant. They did it through modifying existing restaurant operation management procedures, taking them to a new height in the process, to meet KFC's super-fast growth in China. They did it through rolling up their sleeves to show their local colleagues how restaurant operations are done in markets outside China. They did it through setting up internal training programs of varying lengths on diverse topics from basic restaurant operational skills to leadership skills. Eventually, KFC's "Taiwan Gang" also contributed to the development of China's restaurant industry by sharing their experience, expertise, and knowledge with Chinese media, trade associations, government agencies and, through them, with direct and indirect competitors in the Chinese restaurant industry.

Responsibility for the management of a restaurant and its employees is in the hands of the restaurant general manager and members of the management staff. It is not unusual for a KFC restaurant to employ 100 employees or more, including full-time and part-time staff. While the management team of each new KFC restaurant is always composed of experienced KFC restaurant operators, members of the work crew are usually recruited a few weeks in advance of a new restaurant opening. Training for new crew members is the responsibility of the restaurant general manager and the management team. It usually begins a few weeks before a new restaurant opening. Sometimes training takes place inside the new restaurant prior to the grand opening ceremony. At other times, training takes place in another KFC restaurant nearby, as the new restaurant undergoes last-minute preparations for its grand opening such as equipment installation, cleanup, and safety inspection.

After a new restaurant opens for business, on-the-job training for the newly recruited crew continues inside the restaurant. If all goes well, this new restaurant may well become a training restaurant months later for the management team and the work crew of additional new restaurants. With over 2,000 KFC restaurants in China at the beginning of 2008, and five or more managers per restaurant – a restaurant general manager, a deputy general manager, two or more assistant general managers, and a few management trainees – it is not hard to see the magnitude of training infrastructure required in order to meet the demand of KFC restaurant growth in China.

Almost all newly recruited management trainees for future restaurant management development are college or university graduates, many of whom eventually rise to become restaurant general managers and beyond. Today, 80 percent of KFC restaurant general managers in China have a college degree. This is highly unusual in a cultural environment where a career in the restaurant industry has been traditionally frowned upon, if not looked down on, by society at large. At least three factors have contributed to this unusual phenomenon. First, KFC has become a highly recognized, if not highly regarded, brand in China. Second, KFC has become known for the excellence of its employee training and development program. Third, given its rapid expansion, career growth opportunities for promising employees at KFC are much better than most other employers.

Training for restaurant management staff goes beyond in-restaurant training. In addition to continuous on-the-job training, restaurant management staff are subject to classroom training held in a training center when a management staff member becomes eligible for promotion to the next level. Over the years, KFC China has developed a huge training infrastructure that is well suited to the unique market requirements of China and supportive of KFC China's business strategy, with emphasis on restaurant expansion, speed, service, training, and development.

Led by an experienced restaurant operator-turned-teacher/administrator during the 1990s, only a portion of the teaching staff at the Shanghai training center were full-time. The rest of the teaching staff were part-time or on temporary assignment from their regular, field restaurant operation jobs. All of them had lots of restaurant operations and management experience. The result of this practical, field-oriented training system is reflected in teaching materials continuously being upgraded based on current events, issues, and challenges in the field. Teachers bring their hands-on experience to classrooms addressing current real-life cases, while students receive practical training taught by the most experienced, and the best qualified, from their own lot.

Building A People Development Culture

While restaurant operation training reported to restaurant operations as opposed to human resources (HR) during the 1990s, business, management, and other non-operation functional training took place under the leadership of HR with courses on leadership, seven habits, time management, project management, team building, etc.

Training is an important element behind the success of KFC China. Training, learning, and continuous improvement are integral parts of the company's culture. Senior management personally hosted lunchtime brown-bag sessions open to all employees on topics as diverse as business English, Western values and customs, and management systems of multinational corporations. In addition, heads of different functions hosted lunch-time sessions to introduce their respective functions, plans, issues, and challenges to fellow colleagues, both to educate and to communicate.

With senior management encouragement, HR established a small library in the Shanghai headquarters containing books on business, humanities, literature, travel, and other subjects – some on China, but mostly about the world beyond. By sharing knowledge about the world outside China with local colleagues, it was hoped that over time they would be able to develop a broader, better-balanced, worldly perspective on business, as well as on life.

Another form of employee training and development is job rotation across function and geography. This wasn't always easy given traditional Chinese emphasis on family togetherness and attachment to one's hometown, which can result in a general reluctance to relocate. Historically, one of the greatest lifetime achievements of the head of an extended Chinese family is to be able to claim "five generations living under the same roof!" Temporary training overseas, on the other hand, is highly valued by local employees.

During the past two decades, different surveys have indicated that local Chinese employees highly value the training they receive from their employers. Through formal and informal employee training and development programs, KFC China has been successful with the development, growth, and retention of the management talents needed for rapid restaurant expansion.

Build a Winning Culture

In addition to employee training, the abundance of promotional and career growth opportunities as a result of rapid expansion of KFC restaurants year after year provides another strong contributor to employee motivation. Furthermore, KFC's parent company, YUM! Brands, places heavy emphasis on building a culture of employee recognition. Each year, for example, restaurant general managers are the focus of a multiple-day celebration during which the best performers are publicly recognized. Inside each KFC restaurant, pictures of employees of the month can usually be found on the wall near the counter. Other incentives include STAR (a symbol of superior quality) pins and "thank you" cards to publicly recognize noteworthy employee behavior with a pin and a hand-written thank-you card. Additional examples of this recognition-based company culture abound.

When an employee feels good about himself or herself, that feeling of confidence, excitement, and pride inevitably inspires other employees. Winning, like losing, is contagious.

CONCLUSION

A key driving force behind KFC China's success has been a strong desire to become the best in China, and to do everything better than any other company around. The assembly of an industry-experienced team of entrepreneurs with a deep commitment to, and a thorough understanding of, China provided a strong foundation for success. The introduction of systematic programs to train, develop, motivate, and retain talent further solidified that strong foundation and facilitated restaurant expansion at lightening speed. In the restaurant service industry, like many others, the quality of the management team ranks among the most important of all competitive differentiators. KFC's success in China offers yet another vivid validation.

3

BUSINESS STRATEGY

INTRODUCTION

KFC's business strategy in China can be encapsulated in two words: rapid expansion. Two questions immediately follow: How feasible is this strategy and, if achieved, what benefits does it bring? Regarding the first question, KFC China's leadership team knew, early on, that once a profitable restaurant economic model has been validated, constraint to future growth in the next few decades will come largely from the supply side, not the demand side. At least, not while the Chinese economy continues to move forward at an average growth rate of 8 to 10 percent per year.

Referring to Exhibit 9, while China has managed to contain the growth of its population during the decade between 1994 and 2004 to less than 1 percent due largely to the successful implementation of the "one child" policy, total retail sales more than tripled during the same period to US$675 billion. This is still only approximately 19 percent of the size of the retail market in the U.S., but it is up from 9 percent in 1994. Consumer spending, meanwhile, has grown by a compounded 13 percent per annum during the same period, a direct result of the continuing rise in household income. Economists predict that in the foreseeable future, as household income and

Exhibit 9: Private Consumption vs. Retail Sales In China

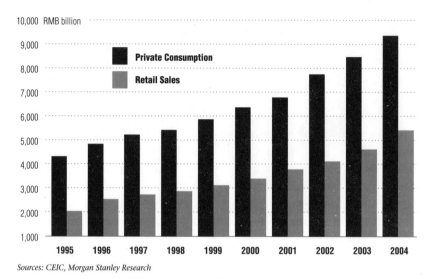

Sources: CEIC, Morgan Stanley Research

consumer spending in general continue to rise, consumer spending on eating out will rise at an even faster pace.

Not surprisingly, China's restaurant industry revenue has been growing between 15–20 percent per year during the same period between 1994 and 2004. The rate of growth of the fast-food segment was even higher during the same period. As the leader of both the fast-food segment (KFC) and the casual-dining segment (Pizza Hut), YUM! Brands China's stated goal of growing at a rate of 22 percent per annum in the foreseeable future seems within reason at first glance, especially in light of its most recent growth record. In 2006, YUM! Brands China's revenue grew 31 percent compared to the year prior. In 2007, once again, 31 percent revenue growth over the prior year.

On the second question, what benefit does this strategy of rapid growth bring? In a single phrase, it's economies of scale.

ECONOMIES OF SCALE

Being the biggest restaurant chain in China gives KFC advantages in cost and prestige. On cost, with more than twice the number of restaurants compared to its closest competitor, KFC has a much bigger volume base than McDonald's to spread fixed expenses such as office rent, headquarters personnel, and advertising. Scale economy also produces huge amount of savings in the supply chain, ranging from material procurement to transportation logistics. KFC and McDonald's in China spend between 35 percent and 50 percent of each RMB of restaurant revenue on the procurement and distribution of raw materials. KFC China's much bigger purchase volume gives it greater scale advantage and negotiation leverage with suppliers, resulting in a comparative cost advantage on a unit-cost basis.

This is assuming that the average revenue generated per KFC and McDonald's restaurant in China is about the same, which is a reasonable, but not probable, assumption in the absence of comparable published data from both sources. According to YUM! Brands' Annual Report, the average KFC restaurant in China delivered RMB10 million, or US$1.2 million, of revenue and a 23 percent restaurant profit margin during 2004. Although comparable figures are not released in McDonald's Annual Report, it would not be surprising if McDonald's comparable figures were noticeably lower. According to estimates, cost advantages attributable to scale, size, and operating efficiencies could have resulted in significant differences in profit margins of up to a whopping 15 percent between KFC and McDonald's in China since McDonald's opened its first restaurant in Shenzhen in 1991.

In addition to cost advantage, being the biggest restaurant chain in China gives KFC a unique brand image in a society where size matters, and a person's "face" – the equivalent of a company's brand image – is all too important. The growing gap in restaurant unit count between KFC and McDonald's is perceived by consumers, government officials, and the media as a reflection of the strengths of the respective brands, further solidifying KFC's leadership image over time.

DURABLE FIRST-MOVER'S ADVANTAGE

KFC's widening lead over McDonald's in the number of restaurants reflects, at least in part, KFC's continual willingness to enter new markets where no other direct competitors dare. By being the first in a new province, city, county, or township, KFC continues to reinforce the public image of being the undisputed industry leader. Being first also means being recognized and appreciated by local government officials whose personal career growth was, at one time, directly tied to local economic growth, ability to attract foreign investment from companies like KFC, and other economic measures. Oftentimes these officials have direct influence over decisions such as how fast (or slow) to approve the license applications for a new company and a new restaurant, which attractive locations are available for lease – and at what price. As a result, KFC's early entry into a new territory often results in competitive advantages in restaurant location, cost, and speed of government approvals in surprising ways.

The first few restaurants in a new territory not only enjoy competitive advantages including restaurant location, cost, prestige, and a smooth relationship with local government officials, but internal KFC China data have demonstrated time and again that the first few restaurants also generate above-average revenues and profits compared to other late-coming KFC restaurants of the same size in the same territory.

DEVELOPING A STRUCTURED APPROACH TO RESTAURANT GROWTH

KFC China's leadership team was not only aware of the impact of scale and size on cost advantage and brand differentiation, it was also keenly aware of the strategic importance of speed, and that in the foreseeable future, the number of KFC restaurants would be constrained largely by resource availability, not by market demand. In pursuing the strategy of rapid growth, KFC structured the timing and sequencing of new market penetration based on two general principles: from east to west, and from hub to hub.

From East to West

From its first restaurant in Beijing, KFC stayed on China's east coast until 1995, opening new markets as far north as Shenyang, Liaoning Province in China's northeast, and as far south as Guangzhou in

Guangdong Province. KFC first expanded away from China's east coast in 1995 when it entered Wuhan, Hubei Province in central China and Chengdu, Sichuan Province in western China. In the ensuing five years, KFC continued its expansion along the eastern coast, marching to the far northern reaches of Harbin near the Russian border, the far eastern offshore islands of Chongming and Zhoushan, and the far southern island of Hainan. More importantly, KFC continued with its aggressive westward expansion deep into China's inland. Today, KFC restaurants are found in all provinces and their administrative equivalent throughout China except Tibet.

KFC's geographic expansion during its first ten years in China was driven primarily by economics, government policies, and local market infrastructure. Economically, the first provinces and cities in China that were opened up to foreign capital for economic experimentation during the initial stage of China's economic reforms were located along China's eastern coast. As a result, China's first wave of emerging middle class – KFC's most attractive target market segment – were mostly found up and down China's eastern coast. Equally important, because they were the first to be targeted by China's central government for economic reforms, provinces and cities along the eastern coast were also the first to adopt more innovative and flexible economic policies, and first to strengthen local economic infrastructures such as roads, airports, and electricity in order to attract foreign direct investment (FDI).

From Hub to Hub

Whenever KFC enters a new province, the first restaurant almost always opens in the provincial capital city, which usually has a big population and the best infrastructure available in that province. Entries in the next largest cities in the same province and neighboring provinces follow closely behind. If a distribution center for supply storage and delivery did not already exist within a driving range that allowed 24-hour turnaround, then a new distribution center would be developed and put into operation before the first restaurant opening. These distribution centers are usually located in the suburbs of a hub city in order to minimize costs associated with warehouse rental and labor, as well as time wasted going in and out of the city center.

Each of these new city markets then becomes a hub, the center for a concentric circle or, more precisely, a series of concentric circles wherein future restaurants are planted. Often, depending on internal resource availability, simultaneous entries in multiple major population centers in a given province are planned and executed. As is always the case, before KFC enters a new market, all elements of a full-functioning supply chain from warehousing and logistics to supply sources for all food and non-food categories – especially local supply for food items of short shelf-life such as vegetables, bread, and dairy products – are already put in place. Each of these items requires months, if not years, of planning and preparation in advance.

The underlying structure of KFC's geographic expansion is driven not only by economics, consumer characteristics, government relations, and supply chain, but also by branding and logistics-related issues. KFC restaurants in large population centers not only attract local consumers, but also out-of-town visitors from surrounding counties, townships, and villages, exposing them earlier than otherwise to the KFC brand, thus paving the way for future expansion into smaller cities and townships. Big population centers are also more likely to be connected to other big population centers through adequate roadways, thereby reducing the time and expense required for restaurant delivery from a distribution center. Once two hub cities are connected through the same distribution center, additional cities, counties, and townships along the way become natural target locations for future restaurant expansion.

Cross-organizational Implications of a Rapid Growth Strategy

Being an industry pioneer with a strategic intent to grow as fast as resources and capabilities allow in a market unconstrained by the volume of opportunities has broad internal, as well as external, organizational implications. Within KFC China, growing as rapidly as resources and capabilities allow stretches every single function, line, and staff, to varying degrees. Functions most affected by this strategy include restaurant operations; new market and restaurant real estate development; HR, especially on employee recruiting, training, and development; distribution and logistics; supply chain management;

and QA. Other functions such as new product development, marketing, finance and accounting, and government and public relations are also stretched continuously, albeit to a lesser extent.

Suppliers of nearly all product categories, from food supplies to restaurant construction materials, furniture, and equipment, and all service categories, from restaurant interior design to mystery shoppers, are directly affected. The challenge facing suppliers is not too different from that facing KFC China: how to grow as fast as resources and capabilities allow in order to meet KFC's growth demands without shortchanging quality and efficiency? Some suppliers do face one additional challenge: how to effectively control single-customer risk as KFC's share of their total company revenue base continues to rise over time, often by leaps and bounds?

In this high-growth environment, efficient internal and external planning, communication, coordination, and exchange of data in a timely manner are critical to successful implementation. Every year the number of planned new restaurants and their locations drive the resource planning process, including the all-important annual operating budget process. Once a new restaurant plan, including schedule of openings, for a new year is in place, finance is able to develop a revenue forecast, taking into consideration historical data, general economic forecasts, and assumptions; restaurant operations is able to develop its staffing, recruiting, and training plans; supply chain management is able to estimate supply volumes and coordinate with all suppliers on the volume and timing of delivery; logistics and distribution is able to forecast if warehousing and trucking capacity needs expansion and, if so, where, when, and by how much; and suppliers can proceed with their initial annual production planning by product type, timing, and geography.

While the strategy – and the rationale behind the strategy – for rapid restaurant growth is straightforward, its actual implementation requires a well-tested system to execute the plan to precision, year after year, through coordinated efforts of many organizations and people, both internal and external. It requires a recognition of the need to develop a system and a process, a discipline to live by such a system and process once in place, and minimum human intervention in their implementation. It also requires a new approach to problem solving through collaborative effort in a time-critical and efficient manner, tearing down walls built around different internal functional silos and external barriers with suppliers, joint venture partners, and others in the process. It requires an open, results-driven company culture focused on meeting or exceeding business objectives with speed, quality, and efficiency.

An Accidental Stimulant for Accelerated Expansion

Ironically, one of the indirect causes for an acceleration of the already rapid growth of new KFC restaurant openings was a push by YUM! Brands' corporate headquarters to reduce overhead expenses after the Asian financial crisis of 1997–1998 brought a decline to KFC's business volume in China. Expenses attributable to expatriate employees accounted for a significant portion of the overhead expenses at the time, and attracted unusual scrutiny. Instead of agreeing to immediate and significant reduction of expatriate expenses, YUM! Brands Greater China counter-proposed a plan to accelerate the speed of opening new restaurants so that fixed overhead expenses would shrink faster over time as a percentage of growing revenues and profits. In the end, a decision to grow as fast as resources and capabilities allowed – people, restaurant sites, cash for reinvestment, and supply chain – turned out to be an optimal strategy. The net result is that KFC China achieved cost leadership through scale, and competitive differentiation through size, speed, and brand recognition.

While doggedly pursuing a business strategy of relentless push for restaurant expansion since the 1990s in order to achieve scale economy, KFC has also deliberately pursued two other strategic initiatives to aid in its attempt to build sustainable competitive advantage. One is branding, part of its overall localization efforts. The other is resource sharing with sister brands. Both strategic initiatives are unique in comparison with KFC's competitors, and have contributed to its leadership position in terms of brand perception and financial performance.

BRAND POSITIONING: AN AMERICAN BRAND WITH CHINESE CHARACTERISTICS

An American brand with Chinese characteristics; a statement reminiscent of the Chinese economic system being described as "a socialist market economy" or "a market economy with socialist characteristics."

There is no point denying the origin of KFC. It is American. However, are "Chinese characteristics" good for KFC, and if so, what is the optimal balance between its American origin and its "Chinese characteristics?" What traits, American and Chinese, constitute an ideal mix in the eyes of the target Chinese consumers? In reality, from the moment the "Taiwan Gang" was first assembled, it became inevitable that KFC China would develop its own Chinese characteristics. This makes sense for at least two reasons. First, the very act of building KFC as an American brand with Chinese characteristics takes advantage of one of KFC's competitive differentiators against other Western competitors – a deep understanding of the Chinese market context. Second, the majority of Chinese consumers are more likely to be drawn to this mixed brand position instead of a purely Western one. As explained in Chapter 1, since the 19th century the average Chinese citizen has been exposed to mixed emotions of admiration and resentment, respect and fear, love and hate toward the West and all things Western. Selling Western products in China can be both a blessing and a curse.

RESOURCE SHARING ACROSS BRANDS

Not many people in China know that KFC and Pizza Hut, another very successful restaurant brand in China, are part of the same company. This has not stopped cross-brand resource sharing between KFC and Pizza Hut as the opportunities for doing so are abundant. For example, KFC and Pizza Hut China's headquarters used to share the same office building in Shanghai. Likewise, the same purchasing function used to handle the procurement for food, kitchen equipment, construction materials, furniture, signage, and other goods and services for both brands. Not only does the combined effort in purchasing save labor and administrative expenses, their combined purchase volume, which is often sourced from the same suppliers, generates incremental volume discounts for both brands. KFC and Pizza Hut restaurants can be found in the same shopping malls, sometimes next to each other, generating leverage on both rental costs and the most attractive restaurant locations when negotiating joint lease agreements.

Another significant opportunity for sharing resources across brands is in sharing management talent, although this is not as obvious as it might seem at first. For restaurant operation management talent, for example, a lot of restaurant management concepts and skills are not directly transferable between these two brands because Pizza Hut in China is positioned as a casual-dining concept instead of a fast-food concept, unlike Pizza Hut in the rest of the world. Employee, skill, and capability transfer between KFC and Pizza Hut works much more smoothly and happens a lot more often in non-operation functions. At the end of 2006, there were over 250 Pizza Hut restaurants in China, rising to over 350 by the end of 2007, and growing rapidly. As both brands continue to expand, competitors will increasingly feel the combined force of this duo in the years ahead.

Yet another area for strategic resource sharing across brands is found, somewhat surprisingly, in new products. For example, roasted chicken wings began as a very popular item on Pizza Hut's menu and eventually ended up on KFC's menu as well. Another example, Portuguese egg tarts, began on KFC's menu and later migrated to Pizza Hut. In the future, such cross-brand product resource sharing will rise by geometric proportion as a third brand that is focused on Chinese fast food, East Dawning, receives heavy investment for new Chinese product development while KFC and Pizza Hut continue on their trail of product localization and proliferation.

BUILDING SUSTAINABLE COMPETITIVE ADVANTAGE

The ultimate aim of a successful competitive strategy is in the creation of sustainable competitive advantage. With it comes superior financial performance. It begins with a strategy to differentiate, in cost and/or other industry key success factors. It ends with successful implementation based on the full commitment of a company and its resources. Invariably, the most challenging test comes in the phase of implementation. KFC China is no exception. While its strategy is straight-forward – growing the number of restaurants as fast as resources and capabilities allowed – its full and successful implementation is one giant, complex task requiring the cooperation of many companies, functions, and people. Among others, successful implementation of KFC China's strategy of rapid restaurant expansion requires, not in any order of priority, these resources and capabilities:

- A continuous supply of qualified people talents, especially experienced restaurant management talents.
- Good, innovative "products" that meet the changing needs of target customer segments, including not only good-tasting food, but also restaurant dining environment, cleanliness and service.
- A proven capability to form business and political partnerships, and to effectively leverage partners' resources, especially in its early days when going direct was not an option due to constraints imposed by the Chinese government.
- A supplier base that is willing and able to invest in new technology and production capacity in order to meet KFC's continuing demand for high quality, high volume growth, and on-time delivery, at a competitive cost.
- A distribution and logistics capability that can be deployed to expand to any new market and overcome any new challenge, at a competitive cost, any time.
- A proven real estate development capability that enables a continuous supply of new restaurant sites, with high capture rate and high hit ratio.
- A company culture that focuses on results, quality, speed, efficiency, innovation, and flexibility.
- An experienced and competent on-the-ground leadership team with a strong sense of time urgency, a capacity for quick decision making, and a propensity for action, innovation, and flexibility based on market and competitive dynamics, backed by a committed and supportive corporate office.

Together, these resources and capabilities represent the key elements behind the successful execution of KFC's strategy in China.

CONCLUSION

Each resource and capability mentioned above is a key success factor that supports the primary strategy of rapid restaurant expansion. Each capability requires a number of systems, processes, resources, skills, and expertise that are linked to, and dependent on, each other. For example, a continuous supply of people talents requires systems and processes for employee recruitment, training and development, management by objectives, performance evaluation, career planning, and management succession planning, all of which are linked to, and have a direct impact on, building other functional capabilities. The importance of each capability is easy to understand, perhaps even easy to imitate, but by itself, insufficient in bringing the overall strategy to reality. Together, they become the engines for a super-fast growth machine that's powerful and virtually impossible to duplicate. Perhaps a much livelier analogy is that, together, like different human body organs, they create a living, thriving human being, with a soul.

Therein lies the ultimate secret behind KFC China's success.

4

LOCAL PARTNERSHIP, GOVERNMENT RELATIONS, AND CRISIS MANAGEMENT

INTRODUCTION

In 2004, once the need to be part of a joint venture was no longer a government requirement, according to official Chinese government statistics over 60 percent of newly approved foreign retailers chose a wholly owned legal structure. In 1987, the year KFC opened its first restaurant in China, there were very few wholly foreign owned enterprises (WFOEs) in China, since WFOEs were not allowed by the government. In fact, through the early 1990s most foreign enterprises making a direct investment to set up operations in China could do so only through joint ventures with local Chinese companies. Since nearly 100 percent of all Chinese companies were still in the hands of the state in the late 1980s, a foreign company's joint venture partner(s) were invariably tied, in one way or another, to various levels of the Chinese government – central, provincial, city, county, and township.

Within this framework of foreign investment, picking the right local joint venture partner(s) became an important policy decision that often determined the success or failure of a foreign investment. A productive local partner could bring not only in-depth knowledge about the local market and government bureaucracy, but also the all-important *guanxi*, or business and political connections. The latter was particularly crucial in the days prior to the 1990s when application and approval processes for business licenses and certificates needed for operation were complex and time-consuming, often requiring months and even years to work through the maze of government bureaucracy.

JOINT VENTURES

Generally speaking, KFC picked the right joint venture partners in China, beginning with Beijing, and later Shanghai. KFC Beijing, the first joint venture company KFC established in China, had more than one joint venture partner, including a state-owned bank and a food distributor/retailer. KFC's joint venture partners in Shanghai were led by New Asia Group, which was later merged into the Jinjiang Group, a huge hotel and catering group of companies that, to this day, remains closely affiliated with the Shanghai Municipal Government. Other joint ventures around Shanghai, including Suzhou, Wuxi, and Hangzhou, followed similar patterns. The local partners of these joint ventures share two common characteristics. First, they are government or pseudo-government enterprises. Second, at least one local partner in each joint venture is already in the food distribution and/or retailing business. As a result, these local partners were able to contribute ready-to-use physical assets and *guanxi* of various categories to a joint venture, thereby facilitating relatively smooth startups and early business success.

The local Chinese joint venture partners provided significant, if not pivotal, contributions not only in getting KFC through a complex maze of government licensing and regulatory hurdles, but also in a multitude of other ways. These include: accessing prime restaurant locations at a discounted price; accessing existing logistics and distribution infrastructure and facilities; accessing existing local suppliers; and even accessing local labor. Back in those days every Chinese worker was affiliated with a *danwei*, or government work unit. Many of them were reluctant to venture away from the protection provided by their *danwei* under the old "iron-bowl" system into a foreign joint venture company for fear of losing cheap housing, heavily subsidized utilities, children's education, health care coverage, retirement benefits, and other state-provided social benefits. Above all, the brave new world of a foreign joint venture company is one without job security, full of risks from the unknown. Without assistance from the local joint venture partners who know their way around the system, KFC's start-up efforts through the first half of the 1990s would have been met with far more surprises, if not setbacks, and would have taken much longer.

Despite the benefits brought to the table by KFC's local joint venture partners, a joint venture agreement can last as long as 20 years, which is a long time for a marriage between two individuals across cultural, political, social, linguistic, and other boundaries, let alone two companies, with all of the dynamic complexities and changes within each enterprise over time. Indeed, managing relationships with joint venture partners was one of the most challenging tasks KFC faced.

During those years, every time KFC tried to promote system-wide standardization projects of any kind, joint venture partners were usually the most difficult to convince. These projects ranged from building an efficient supply chain based on the adoption of a system-wide, common quality standard, to consolidating warehouse facilities in order to gain system-wide efficiency.

The source of such uneasy relationships with joint venture partners invariably points to self-interest and difference in objectives. Shortly after joining KFC Greater China, I began consolidating the supply chain, and centralizing the purchasing function at the same time. This met with stiff resistance from the field, and the strongest resistance came from the joint venture partners. For years prior to the consolidation, these joint venture markets had developed some suppliers on their own, separate from the rest of the KFC system. Many of those suppliers shared common government lineage with local joint venture partners and, in some cases, had developed close personal ties. In almost all cases, breaking these ties unilaterally would mean breaking long-standing *guanxi* – losing "face" in the process. In other cases, joint venture partners made business arrangements with a given supplier, and a severance of the business relationship would result in a direct, immediate, and unfavorable economic impact – something to be avoided at all costs.

Other causes for strained relationships between KFC and joint venture partners varied from incongruence of long-term goals and business strategies to conflicts of interest. Some local joint venture partners preferred the maximization of near-term profits and the redistribution of at least part of the profits back to shareholders, while KFC preferred reinvestment of profits for accelerated new restaurant growth and brand building. In one situation, a local joint venture partner decided to establish another QSR brand on its own while the joint venture agreement with KFC was still in force. Although this QSR chain was not focused on chicken products and did not compete directly against KFC, such practices did not contribute to building mutual trust.

In the early 1990s, the Chinese government began a renewed effort to attract foreign investment. To do so, the old, cumbersome, time-consuming foreign investment application processes were gradually streamlined throughout China. What used to take years for government authorities to approve began to take months, even weeks. In part to meet entry requirements for the WTO, deregulation began to set in, eventually removing government-imposed requirements for foreign joint ventures in most industries except a few sensitive bastions of holdout such as financial services, telecommunications, energy, media, and defense. The era of joint ventures has since been slowly fading away.

Since the mid-1990s, KFC has not only refrained from entering any new joint venture agreement, but also has actively sought to buy out local partners from existing joint ventures, with some success. These buyouts are based on mutually agreeable terms, with price usually standing out as a deal breaker. As a joint venture agreement edges closer to its natural expiration, KFC's negotiation leverage usually rises.

KFC's experience in China is not unique. According to statistics published by the Chinese government, more and more foreign enterprises investing in China choose WFOEs instead of joint ventures. In fact, between 1996 and 2004, the volume of foreign equity joint venture investments declined steadily from one half of all foreign investments to approximately one quarter, while the volume of foreign wholly owned investments rose from a quarter to two-thirds, as Exhibit 10 illustrates. Beginning in 2005, the Chinese government allowed minority equity investment by foreign banks in local Chinese banks for the first time since 1949, thus distorting, and reversing, a trend of rising WFOEs in investment volume.

Exhibit 10: Foreign Direct Investment (FDI) In China by Type of Enterprise: 1979–2006 (US$)

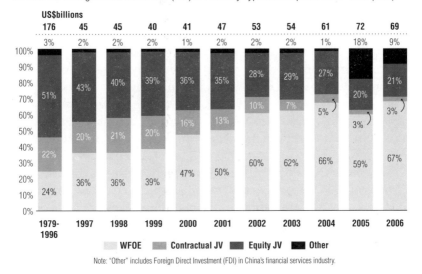

Note: "Other" includes Foreign Direct Investment (FDI) in China's financial services industry.

Source: National Statistics Bureau of China

FRANCHISE

In 1993, KFC signed a non-exclusive franchise agreement with a Taiwanese gentleman who brought with him a business case based on local connections and prior industry experience. The franchise territory under discussion covered Xian, the capital city of Shaanxi Province in northwest China, and the surrounding areas. Xian is home to the world-famous Terracotta Army of Qin Shi-Huang, the first emperor who unified China in 221 BC. Xian was also the capital for eleven different dynasties throughout Chinese history, including the Western Han Dynasty (206 BC – 5 AD) and the Tang Dynasty (618 AD – 907 AD). Rich in history and aging glory, Xian in modern times had been fading in colors until the end of the last century when a national push to develop China's west was announced by the State Council. Since then, Xian has regained its strategic importance as the gateway to China's west. In the early 1990s, however, despite its international fame as a tourist city, Xian was not a focal point for economic development in the eyes of the Chinese central government or, for that matter, foreign investors. KFC knew this. Furthermore, in the foreseeable future, KFC would be busy cultivating bigger, strategically more important, and financially more rewarding markets up and down the eastern coast of China, with few spare resources available to develop a relatively remote and distant market in Shaanxi. Why not franchise a territory that you yourself have no plan to develop on your own in the near future, both as an offensive and a defensive strategic move? A franchise agreement was struck. Years passed and Xian KFC survived the economic hardship of the early, pioneering days, while actually growing in volume and profits with its own warehouse, supply chain, and other necessary ingredients of a functioning restaurant chain. Fully functioning? Yes. Up to KFC China standard? Probably not. Over the years, KFC Xian has cooperated on many programs initiated by KFC China, generally at a slower pace, requiring a gentle push from time to time, and an occasional jolt into action from KFC Restaurant Support Center in Shanghai. It has not been an ideal work relationship. Once again, as in the case of joint venture partners, causes for a strained business relationship can be traced back to differences in business objectives and conflict of economic interests.

In more recent years, as the franchise agreement for each KFC restaurant in Xian approached expiration, negotiation for franchise extension or for the franchisee to sell its KFC restaurants back to KFC China failed time and again, primarily due to the gap between the price offered by KFC and the price expected by the franchisee. This contributed to a deterioration of the work relationship to a point where, in 2004, KFC China began opening its own restaurants in Shaanxi Province separately and independently from those operated by the franchisee, re-walking the same path found in Taiwan during the 1990s.

There was not to be another KFC franchisee until the arrival of the new millennium, details of which will be discussed in Chapter 7. By then, KFC had learned a lesson from Xian, and adopted a different approach to franchising in China. Never again will KFC China knowingly franchise a geographic territory, no matter how small or remote.

OWNERSHIP BLIND

In the face of these sources of tension between KFC and its joint venture and franchise partners, it's not surprising that I found an ambivalent attitude toward both among employees in the China headquarters when I first joined YUM! Brands in 1997. This must change, I said to myself. Of course, I wanted to rebuild and strengthen the work relationship with joint venture and franchise partners out of mutual business interests, but I was driven primarily by the conviction that KFC customers should not be able to tell any difference between a company-owned versus a partner-owned KFC restaurant; nor should they care. All KFC restaurants in China, be they 100 percent company-owned, 100 percent franchisee-owned, or jointly owned through a joint venture, should present a single "face," a consistent, high-quality image, to the public. As a corollary, all KFC restaurants must follow the same high standard in presenting the same appearance in perception and the same satisfying dining experience to customers everywhere in China. To achieve these goals, employees of KFC, especially those working out of the Restaurant Support Center in Shanghai, must adopt an "ownership-blind" attitude in our response to field requests for guidance and assistance, and in providing service and support.

An example needed to be set. If two markets, one company-owned and the other a joint venture, called simultaneously for help with an emergency supply shortage, the latter would enjoy higher priority for a change. Pretty soon, joint venture and franchisee partners took notice of a difference in the timeliness and quality of headquarters response to their requests. Trust, confidence, and, eventually, day-to-day work relationships between employees of KFC China and its partners slowly improved.

GOVERNMENT RELATIONS

Part of the change brought by China's economic reforms lies in the growing awareness and consensus within senior levels of the central government that the primary role for government in the business sector should be to establish the rules of the game, step outside the ring, and return as an adjudicator of conflicts only when it's absolutely necessary. Nevertheless, compared to governments elsewhere, even today the Chinese government still retains great control and exercises great influence over an average business enterprise's destiny when it chooses to. It's no surprise, then, to find foreign companies in China placing more weight, even today, on government relations than public relations. Nor is it a surprise to find foreign companies in China without a public relations function until recent years, while a government relations function has been in place since day one.

One of the unexpected benefits brought by KFC's joint venture in Shanghai is a well-managed government relations program at its Shanghai headquarters. Early on, through assistance from New Asia Group, KFC's joint venture partner in Shanghai, KFC China recruited a native Shanghainese who was very knowledgeable about the food industry, had lots of industry and government contacts, and, most importantly, was very well-versed in Chinese politics. While keeping a low profile, he has over the years been officially responsible for KFC China's government relations program. Unofficially, he has been KFC's internal consultant on a broad range of thorny issues involving government agencies, joint venture partners, and the news media. Every time a government bottleneck needs to be cleared, a hard-line joint venture partner's position needs to be softened, or a broken relationship needs to be mended, he has been able to work his way through a myriad of situations to bring solutions to these problems.

Of all KFC China's local employees, this man made the most valuable contributions to KFC China's success over the years. Displaying many traits valued by Chinese intellectuals through the ages, he is a humble, wise, skillful, and relationship-oriented Chinese gentleman.

During KFC China's first decade, when business scale was still small and organizational structure was loosely decentralized, relationships with various provincial, city, and local government units within each market were managed by each market general manager. In the late 1990s, when a separate government and public relations function was established in all KFC markets, dedicated personnel were committed to this function. Led by the Shanghai headquarters, a systematic, China-wide structure and process began to evolve in order to more effectively manage all external relations. A crisis management system was one of the direct results of this effort.

CRISIS MANAGEMENT

During the mid-1990s, YUM! Brands Greater China seemed to experience a continuing stream of crises, mostly of the nature of a market running out of supply of some kind, usually something critical to revenue generation such as chicken, cooking oil, etc. As the number of restaurants grew, incidents such as robberies inside KFC restaurants and on the roadway when KFC trucks made their restaurant deliveries began to surface. Other incidents such as customer complaints or accidents taking place inside restaurants were also on the rise. These and other crises of varying nature, some of which had internal operation and support implications, others with public relations implications, all needed to be managed quickly, effectively, and systematically.

The most effective approach to crisis management begins with crisis prevention, based on scenario planning, documentation, and clear and broad communication of the procedures, players, responsibilities, authorities, and accountabilities in handling different types of crises likely to occur before they actually take place. KFC wanted to get a crisis management program up and running in order to build, over time, a comprehensive system and capability to deal effectively with various crises, especially the most probable and the most damaging of them.

Sudden Explosion

The first major test of KFC China's crisis management capabilities came without the slightest hint of any kind. In fact, the cause for the crisis had nothing whatsoever to do with KFC. It happened on May 8, 1999, a Saturday. Earlier that week the YUM! Brands Greater China Executive Committee held a number of KFC and Pizza Hut business planning and review meetings, first in Hong Kong and later that week in Taiwan. The meetings ended Friday afternoon in Taipei. Early the next morning I flew to Beijing via Hong Kong on the first flight out, a journey that I had to make frequently during the previous two decades and dreaded each time because of the waste of time and money. For political reasons the government of Taiwan has steadfastly refused for decades to allow direct commercial flights between the Chinese mainland and this offshore island, separated by a narrow strait. The net result is that all flights had to go through Hong Kong, Macau, Okinawa, or some other port outside the Chinese mainland, turning an otherwise two-hour direct flight into a nearly full-day saga.

Upon landing in Beijing that afternoon, I proceeded straight to the oldest KFC restaurant in China, Qianmen KFC, which is located next to Tiananmen Square, to review the plan for a major interior renovation project that would add quite a bit of local color to its internal decor through the display of traditional Chinese art pieces of various forms, such as flying kites, pottery figurines, and paper cuttings. When the taxi cruised past Beijing's foreign embassy district, I was shocked by what I had never seen before in my years of travel throughout China up to that point.

What appeared in my view was a stream of well-organized street demonstrators marching on the sidewalk outside the embassy walls. Many of the marchers were wearing red headbands, while all of them shouted angry slogans, with some defiant fists raised in the air. At the front of the line was a wide red banner with one pole on each end held by a few of the demonstrators. From a distance, I could vaguely make out the Chinese characters for the word "atrocity." As it turned out, at 5:45 AM earlier that day, the Chinese embassy in Belgrade, Yugoslavia, was bombed by several American missiles. Three Chinese journalists died and a score of Chinese diplomats were injured. I called Shanghai Restaurant Support Center immediately, by which time all KFC restaurants in China, over 300 of them, were already in a crisis management mode.

Over the course of the ensuing days, public demonstrations in front of U.S. consulates and U.S. business enterprises such as KFC and McDonald's in Beijing, Shanghai, Chengdu, Changsha, Xian, Shenyang, Hangzhou, Xiamen, and other cities throughout China broke out. In response, some KFC restaurants were temporarily shut down after first covering up the exterior signage and removing moveable objects – especially the statue of Colonel Sanders, which had been mistaken by some demonstrators as Uncle Sam – from sight in order to prevent break-ins and acts of vandalism. Police were called in at some KFC restaurants where large crowds had gathered after a few KFC restaurants had been sacked by angry crowds. Employees of KFC were instructed to leave the restaurants that had been shut down.

In the end, KFC China survived this crisis with minimum employee injury and physical damage, passing the first major test of its crisis management capability.

By the time KFC's Beijing Qianmen store reopened on June 24, 1999, things had returned to normal.

In a January 2008 election, the Nationalist Party regained control of Taiwan's Parliament. Two months later, a Nationalist Party candidate won the presidential election. As a result, direct commercial flights between mainland China and Taiwan will, at long last, resume after sixty years.

Perfecting Crisis Management

Since 1999, KFC China has worked to refine its crisis management system and capabilities. Today, there is a comprehensive system in place within each KFC market and in the Shanghai Restaurant Support Center, to deal with crises of varying nature. Judging from the way KFC responded to the severe acute respiratory syndrome (SARS) crisis in 2003, the avian flu crisis in 2004, the Sudan 1 red-dye crisis, and the avian flu crisis in 2005, KFC's crisis management system is working very well, despite the very significant and immediate – sometimes lasting – impact each of these crises has brought to KFC China in terms of revenue and profit lost and damage done to the brand image.

Throughout 2003, when SARS became such a scare that many foreign business people postponed or stopped traveling to China, KFC continued its restaurant expansion. In fact, over 230 new restaurants opened in China during 2003, reflecting a slight growth over the previous year. This is not at all surprising. After all, the Asian financial crisis in 1997–1998 did not cause a slowdown in KFC's restaurant growth either. As a matter of fact, many in KFC at the time believed that the brand should grow even more aggressively in times of economic slowdown, when many competitive brands are hesitant to expand, leaving new and attractive markets and restaurant sites less contested, and less expensive, for KFC to acquire.

The official Xinhua news agency announced the first confirmed case of avian flu found in China on January 27, 2004. KFC China first learned of this news at dawn on that day. By early afternoon, after a national conference call with all KFC markets participating and the Shanghai Restaurant Support Center presiding, a national press statement was issued announcing that all of KFC China's chicken supplies came from areas outside the infected region. On the following day, KFC released in major news media throughout China a series of anticipated questions and answers from consumers regarding the continual consumption of its chicken products. Shortly after that, TV commercials emphasizing KFC's germ-cleansing, high-temperature cooking process and other safety measures to render the flu-carrying agent's survival hopeless started appearing across China, replacing existing TV commercials. Throughout this period, only the public relations department of YUM! Brands China's Shanghai Restaurant Support Center was authorized to make any public statement and to respond to any public enquiry.

At the same time, KFC instituted the following programs focused on its product menu and supply chain, the news media, the consuming public, and even the Chinese government. First, KFC required all its poultry suppliers to certify that all KFC products came from uninfected areas and had passed government safety inspections. Second, a series of non-chicken products were introduced including pork, seafood, and vegetables. Third, news conferences were held in each KFC market in China and news reporters were invited to local KFC restaurants to sample KFC's chicken products. Fourth, KFC released, for the first time, select parameters surrounding the cooking process of its chicken products, such as minimum cooking times at a temperature of 160 degrees Celsius. Fifth, KFC invited food safety and nutritional experts to go to KFC restaurants to sample its chicken products and to testify that under KFC's cooking procedures, no flu agent could possibly survive. Sixth, KFC even invited Chinese government officials, most notably a deputy minister of commerce, to sample its chicken products in a KFC restaurant in Beijing, which became a piece of red-hot national news overnight.

CONCLUSION

KFC faced a very different market environment in China at the time of its entry compared to other markets around the world, starting with the omnipresence of government and the necessity for joint ventures. Instead of slowing down or backing out, KFC made the best of these and other obstacles, leveraging their forces whenever possible, turning each lemon into lemonade. This knack for being flexible and creative paved the way for its success in a dynamic and unpredictable market environment, from partner selection to crisis management, from government relations to public relations, and from product design to brand marketing.

5

PRODUCT AND MARKETING

INTRODUCTION

There are three natural advantages that KFC enjoys over McDonald's in China when it comes to products. First, Chinese the world over love food prepared deep-fried. Second, Chinese the world over love chicken. Not as much as pork, but chicken is definitely more preferred by Chinese than beef, mutton, fish, or seafood. Third, most Chinese I know who have tried KFC's Original Recipe like its taste – granted this conclusion is not based on a statistically valid random sample.

As can be seen from Exhibit 11, despite the three general statements made above, food preferences and habits across China vary a lot. The differences are driven by factors such as climate, terrain, native crops, ethnicity, and religion. Generally speaking, pork is most preferred everywhere except Ningxia, Qinghai, and Xinjiang, where beef and mutton are preferred due to the concentration of Muslims and ethnic minorities. All three are located in western China, with a combined population of approximately two percent of China's total of 1.3 billion. In the rest of China, pork reigns supreme with no exception. Between chicken and beef/mutton, of the remaining 24 provinces and autonomous regions, eight of them – accounting

Exhibit 11: Per Capita Meat Consumption in Urban Households

Northern Provinces	Pork (Kg)	Beef & Mutton (Kg)	Poultry (Kg)	Population (M)
Gansu	12.8	6.9	2.2	25.9
Hebei	13.4	3.2	1.4	68.5
Heilongjiang	13.3	3.9	2.8	38.2
Henan	12.8	2.4	5.1	97.7
Inner Mongolia	11.0	6.8	3.2	23.9
Jilin	14.0	3.9	3.1	27.2
Liaoning	16.4	4.6	3.3	42.2
Ningxia	7.5	8.2	4.2	6.0
Qinghai	13.0	13.5	4.4	5.4
Shaanxi	12.1	1.8	3.1	37.2
Shandong	22.5	4.3	8.5	92.4
Shanxi	10.6	2.1	2.0	33.6
Xinjiang	5.1	14.7	6.8	20.1
Tibet	14.5	13.9	5.7	2.8

Southern Provinces

	Pork (Kg)	Beef & Mutton (Kg)	Poultry (Kg)	Population (M)
Anhui	14.1	2.6	8.3	65.2
Fujian	17.2	2.2	6.3	35.3
Guangdong	19.4	2.1	15.6	91.9
Guangxi	21.2	2.4	4.3	49.3
Guizhou	14.0	1.3	6.0	39.3
Hainan	17.8	2.1	13.5	8.3
Hunan	19.5	1.6	7.7	67.3
Hubei	17.1	1.7	3.2	60.3
Jiangsu	18.5	1.6	9.4	74.7
Jiangxi	19.7	1.0	4.9	43.1
Sichuan	18.5	1.9	2.7	87.5
Yunnan	22.5	2.4	6.6	44.5
Zhejiang	14.3	1.0	9.3	49.0

Source: Booz Allen Hamilton

for approximately 20 percent of China's total population – prefer beef and mutton over chicken. The other sixteen, which together account for three-quarters of China's population, prefer chicken over beef and mutton.

PRODUCT LOCALIZATION

Although chicken is preferred over beef by the great majority of Chinese, and KFC's Original Recipe is accepted by most Chinese I have encountered who have tasted it, KFC China did not stop there. In fact, for years the most popular product sold by KFC China was a hot and spicy de-boned thigh, deep-fried and placed in a hamburger bun. KFC China did not stop there either. Today, on KFC China's menu board a consumer can find Chinese-style porridge, a popular morning fare in China, for breakfast; fresh salad for lunch; and Beijing Chicken Roll (a la Beijing Duck!) served with scallion and seafood sauce for dinner. Once again, KFC did not stop there. At the end of 2005, KFC introduced a product called Spicy Diced Chicken, resembling a popular, famous Sichuan-style dish. At the beginning of 2008, KFC introduced *yiu-tiao* (fritters of twisted dough), a quintessentially Chinese breakfast food item. Such product innovations have been going non-stop in the current decade, creating a growing impression that KFC has become ever more localized in its product offerings and, therefore, a more localized company than a Western company.

KFC China's effort toward product expansion and localization began in the late 1990s, when a "test kitchen" was established on the top floor of a KFC restaurant a few minutes walking distance from the China headquarters in Shanghai. The final decision to select this site was based on convenience in more ways than one. First, although the unit rental cost of the selected site was higher than other alternatives, most of which were located inside industrial parks in the suburbs of Shanghai, the fact that it was within a few minutes' walking distance from some of the busiest KFC and Pizza Hut restaurants found in China, as well as the Shanghai Restaurant Support Center, brought enormous benefits. Not the least of which has been the amount of time saved by employees ranging from the senior leadership team to the R&D staff, all of whom are based in the Shanghai Restaurant

Support Center. Second, the test kitchen was located on the top floor of an existing KFC restaurant that, due to the openings of several additional KFC restaurants nearby, had under-utilized restaurant space. Thus, the placement of the test kitchen on the top floor of an existing KFC restaurant brought enhanced utilization of an under-used company asset. Third, the test kitchen was surrounded by four KFC and two Pizza Hut restaurants within a few minutes' walking distance of each other, thus providing a very convenient live setting for market research of new products and new equipment.

As is the case with other industries, while many, if not most, new KFC product ideas do not lead to a product launch or even to a prototype, quite a few of the product ideas do make it to the initial product tasting stage, which is always attended by the R&D staff, and often by KFC China's executive team in those days. To be able to walk across the street from your office into an R&D laboratory where you can taste freshly prepared food or test-market the same food in an operating restaurant nearby on a small scale can save lots of time and money. Occasionally, a new product will require new kitchen equipment to be installed in every single KFC restaurant throughout China, in which case the kitchen equipment layout may have to be realigned, kitchen operating manuals may have to be rewritten, and employees may have to be retrained. Before such a decision of major operational significance is fully implemented, it's ideal to have a laboratory located next to live operating restaurants in which a new piece of equipment can be installed temporarily, where the experimental world and the real-action world are only minutes and yards apart, and the flow of information between them is both direct and immediate.

KFC China's frequent introduction of new and localized products is a direct result of its business strategy, management focus, system and process, supply chain, and a number of other factors. The decision to establish a test kitchen within China at a location within walking distance of its China headquarters brought not only economic efficiency, but also a culture of new product development. This was accomplished through the establishment of a new product development process; frequent and repeated trials and errors on different new product concepts; senior leadership interest, involvement, and time commitment; and bringing R&D closer to the real world of restaurant operation and consumer preference.

McDonald's Product Disadvantage

McDonald's weaker competitive position, as implied by its smaller relative market share and profit margin compared to KFC in China, is not a direct result of its product offerings – not by a decisive margin, anyway. As a matter of fact, many of McDonald's product offerings in China are superior-tasting products. These include the Big Mac, fish burger, fruit pies, French fries, ice cream, and even some of its chicken products. Nor is its problem a total lack of new product innovation. The taro pie introduced at the end of 2005 and the banana pie introduced at the beginning of 2008 are recent examples of good tasting new products. Nevertheless, McDonald's has lagged behind KFC China in the frequency, volume, and speed of new and innovative product introductions coming into the current decade. Furthermore, when McDonald's introduces new products, they are often perceived by Chinese consumers as less local than those from KFC for reasons ranging from consumer brand perception to the comparative frequency, variety, and degree of perceived "localness" of new products introduced by both brands.

Despite this perception, McDonald's China has clearly not been sitting still on new product development and introduction. The strongest evidence comes from the introduction of chicken-based products, and a continuing emphasis on chicken-based products. In recent years, McDonald's has sold more chicken than beef products in Shanghai and other markets in China.

Based on Chinese consumers' dietary preferences, as illustrated in Exhibit 11, many have come to the conclusion that McDonald's is doomed to play Number Two in China. This is not necessarily the case. However, in order for McDonald's to overcome its product disadvantage resulting from Chinese consumers' general preference for chicken over beef, more and better-tasting new products targeting Chinese consumers' preference in combination with a more creative product and market segmentation strategy and implementation will be necessary. This, in turn, will require strong corporate commitment for localization from its worldwide headquarters in Oak Brook, Illinois.

For example, why shouldn't McDonald's introduce a new "product frontier" in order to one-up KFC's product advantage in China through a series of pork-based products? After all, Chinese consumers prefer pork products over both beef and chicken. In the end, over-coming the emotional obstacles over decisions such as this will be far more challenging than overcoming obstacles related to R&D, return on investment, or any other business factor.

MARKET SEGMENTATION, TARGETING, AND DIFFERENTIATION

Between hamburgers and fried chicken, while the former is individu-ally packed, the latter comes in as many different pieces as ordered and is, therefore, better suited for sharing at family and other group occasions such as gatherings of friends, classmates, and co-workers in celebration of a birthday or a "job well done," Chinese New Year, and so on. The average Chinese loves a group gathering around a din-ner table. It is part of their culture. Some Sinologists view the core of Confucianism as not much more than the behavioral guidelines for proper conduct in day-to-day interactions with each other.

The KFC Family Bucket fits neatly into this culture. In 2002, the Family Bucket was finally introduced in China, targeting not only members of a family, but also any social group made up of colleagues, classmates, partygoers, or, indeed, participants in any event at any location where people gather. This move marked a significant step by KFC to broaden its traditional target market segments in China, the timing of which matched very well with KFC's rapid geographic expansion throughout China.

For a long time before the Family Bucket was introduced, KFC China focused on two target market segments: children and youth. Both age groups offer business opportunities for the present as well as the future, with the prospect of decades of direct consumption by these target consumers, plus the influence they will exert on their offspring, friends, and relatives for generations to come. Both age groups are easier to convert to a Western brand such as KFC than older age groups. As is the case in many markets around the world, the youth usually lead in the adoption of the latest fashions, and the children often determine where and when a family goes out to eat. In China, this phenomenon of children and youth playing a pivotal role in select family decisions has been magnified by the one-child policy imposed on urban dwellers since 1979. Under this policy, too many single kids, and teenagers, have too often been spoiled by their family members. This situation is unlikely to be resolved as long as there is a mother, a father, two grandmothers, and two grandfathers competing to pamper you at all times.

Market Segmentation – Rural Versus Urban

As implied in Chapter 1, China is not a homogeneous restaurant market no matter how it is segmented – by geography (eastern China versus western China, or province or city versus county); by economic categories (urban versus rural, job categories, or income level); by occasion (working lunch, birthday party, family gathering, etc.); or by different cuisines. To simplify this discussion, it is useful to focus on the urban-rural dimension for market segmentation, briefly discussing the rural segment, but putting the main emphasis on the urban segment, the bulk of KFC's current market base, in the remainder of this chapter.

At the beginning of 2006, the estimated urban-rural population split in China was roughly 550 million and 750 million, respectively, following three decades of population migration from rural to urban China. In the 1990s, the pace of migration sped up, adding on average five to ten or more million new migrants each year. If the same rate of population migration observed during the 1990s continues, then China will, for the first time in Chinese history, have more urban citizens than rural by the year 2020. Thus far, KFC China has largely been targeting China's urban population, and a big part of KFC China's growth is a result of China's rising urbanization.

At the beginning of 2008, of nearly 700 cities in China, KFC had entered – but not fully penetrated – over 400 of them, most of which are located in eastern China. Chinese consumers living in these cities are the first to be exposed to foreign products and concepts, most able to afford KFC's price, and most likely to be working for foreign or joint venture companies. They have been undergoing an urbanization process not too dissimilar from middle classes the world over. When facing the rising urban middle class in these huge, well-developed metropolis such as Shanghai, Beijing, Shenzhen, Guangzhou and, increasingly, other second-tier, even third and fourth-tier cities, KFC's approach to market segmentation and the development of an appropriate marketing mix to capture prospects and retain customers is not very different from that used in other developed countries around the world. In this instance, KFC is simply fast food, or, to be more precise, one of the many choices of Western fast-food chains available today in most major Chinese cities. Consumers in these cities are driven by the same set of selection criteria that drives consumers the world over when facing a decision on which fast-food restaurant to go to: food selection and flavor, price performance, speed and convenience, service quality, and brand loyalty. Such is not the case in rural China.

In rural China, the arrival of KFC is often viewed by local government officials as a coming of age, and by local consumers as a starry event. It's not unusual to see people queuing up outside the first KFC restaurant in a rural township for an American experience, or passersby stopping for a photo session with the statue of Colonel Sanders. As a matter of fact, the first few KFC restaurants in a new city are often the most profitable of all KFC restaurants in China for this very reason, due largely to the novelty effect. Although changing fast, many of these rural Chinese townships remain years, sometimes decades, behind their big, eastern, urban counterparts in terms of economic development, degree of urbanization, exposure to foreign influence, and consumer sophistication. In these rural markets, consumers are drawn to KFC in the absence of advertising and other costly marketing expenses. Higher business volume combined with lower operating expenses often result in higher profitability. Over time, as these rural economies develop, new competitors enter, and consumer sophistication rises, KFC begins to rely more on traditional marketing mixes such as branding, advertising, promotion, and public relations, thus normalizing restaurant cost structures and profit margins.

Brand Symbols

In addition to its product advantage, KFC China has benefited from the symbol of its brand, Colonel Sanders. For millennia the Chinese have revered their aged. Respecting and honoring the elderly, a symbol of wisdom and good fortune, has been a virtue practiced by the Chinese over the centuries. During the 1980s and throughout the 1990s, there was probably no more effective brand symbol than Colonel Sanders with his natural white hair and long beard, offering a perception of wisdom, affection, and grandfatherly gentleness. It worked. Young children were attracted by the white-haired grandfatherly figure. Parents and grandparents willingly put their trust in the same gentle, grandfatherly figure. KFC's business was boosted by the image of the Colonel. Moreover, the Colonel helped KFC establish a warm, friendly, even family-oriented image in a society where families, not individuals, historically made up the fundamental ingredients for its composition.

In the late 1990s, YUM! Brands corporate headquarters began an internal campaign to raise the profile of Colonel Sanders' cartoon imagery in an attempt to gradually phase out the "live Colonel" in future publicity events, which many believed to be a mistake. Later on, in part to counter Ronald McDonald, Chicky, a fluffy chicken mascot, was introduced as the center of KFC China's advertising and promotional programs targeting children. But for many years before that, the Colonel played a significant and contributory role in building and enhancing a positive, friendly brand image in the eyes of the Chinese consumers across all age brackets.

Differentiation Against McDonald's

As the brand image of KFC China moves closer, in the eyes of Chinese consumers, to a "Western brand with Chinese characteristics" through the introduction of localized new product offerings and advertising, McDonald's brand image in China remains distinctly American. While this brand positioning may be appropriate for McDonald's, given its primary target market segment of the young and fashionable, it is not the best way to position a brand in a country with a recent history of conflicts between traditional Chinese and modern, Western values, coupled with a growing nationalistic sentiment reflective of China's growing economic influence around the globe.

The difference in brand image between KFC and McDonald's as projected through their respective TV advertising has in recent years become more pronounced. While McDonald's continues to focus on the young and hip by stressing individuality and self-expression through the "i'm lovin' it" advertising campaign, relying on young sports and entertainment stars as brand spokespersons, KFC has moved to appeal to a much broader target base covering both young and old by emphasizing family, friends, and colleagues of all ages. KFC's shift away from the days when kids were very much the center of its advertising focus is worth noting. In a way, this broadening of target audience reflects a maturing process for the brand. Not too long ago, almost every new KFC restaurant had set aside reserved corners for children's birthday parties, and specially trained staff, usually young ladies, who would lead young children in singing and dancing following the tunes of Chicky. Today, these scenes are more likely to be found in new KFC restaurants located in the residential neighborhoods of big cities and in third and fourth-tier cities throughout the country. In a big city like Shanghai, one is as likely to see young children as teenagers, grown adults, and the elderly in an average KFC restaurant these days.

Thus, compared to McDonald's, KFC stands out in the eyes of Chinese consumers in at least two ways. First, although both brands are known as American, KFC is perceived as more "Chinese" than McDonald's. Second, KFC is perceived as more mature, family-friendly, and appealing to a broader set of age brackets and more diverse market segments than McDonald's; McDonald's is perceived as more chic, fashionable, individualistic, and focused on the youth market segment.

Differentiation Against Other Foreign Restaurant Chains

Over the years, a number of foreign restaurant chains have entered China. Of these, some have experienced notable success. KFC and McDonald's are the most well known. Pizza Hut, a sister brand of KFC, has also done very well. Other rising foreign restaurant chains in recent years worth noting include Papa John's and several Japanese chains led by Wei-Chien Ramen. None of them competes directly against KFC, nor do any of them enjoy a national presence yet, although that may be changing as these brands expand. Of other Western brands competing against KFC, A&W entered China many years ago through Beijing, failed, and pulled out due largely to the absence of enthusiasm of local taste buds for its core product offerings such as hamburgers, hot dogs, and root beer. Burger King entered

China through Shanghai in 2004 and suffered from organizational tur-
moil, short-term financial focus, poor financial return, and difficulty
in attracting strong franchisee partners. Popeyes Chicken entered and
retreated due to poor restaurant locations and insufficient brand vis-
ibility, and has been rumored to be eying a return since. Wendy's
has so far stayed out of China, probably a good decision in view of
McDonald's and Burger King's track record in China. It took the former nearly a decade before registering its first profit; and four years
after initial market entry, the fate of the latter remains unclear. If
Wendy's ever decided to enter China, it'd better come prepared with
an outstandingly differentiable strategy and, on top of that, it must
pay the price of a latecomer's competitive disadvantage.

Two other brands, neither of which competes directly against KFC,
are worth mentioning. One is Starbucks, which entered China in
1999 and by early 2006 had 220 locations in eighteen cities, divided
among a few regional partners, one of which, The Uni-President
Group, is based in Taiwan and focused on eastern China. Another, a
Hong Kong-based restaurant/catering group, Maxim's, is focused on
southern China. A third is focused on northern China. In addition
to these partnerships, Starbucks has opened wholly owned stores in
other parts of China since 2005. It's interesting to note that Starbucks
has achieved this impressive result in a tea-drinking country, where
the cost of a cup of its coffee is sometimes more than an average Chinese worker's daily wage.

Another brand worth mentioning is Subway, which opened its first
restaurant in Beijing in 1995. It later suffered setbacks with the first few
restaurants in Shanghai through a franchisee who made multiple errors,
including poor site selections, but the chain has done better in Beijing
with over 40 stores. It continues to expand aggressively, with a presence
in over a dozen cities and 80 stores throughout China by 2008.

Generally speaking, China is too big, complex, and dynamic a market to be effectively managed from a distance. Front-end investment
in the set-up of a local team and infrastructure – including restaurant
operation, back office, and supply chain – is a necessary ingredient for
survival. Growth through large-scale franchising without first establishing direct, on-the-ground operational experience is a high-risk
proposition that should be avoided. In the end, it's better not to enter
China than to enter China haphazardly.

Differentiation Against Local Restaurant Chains

While KFC is positioned as a more local brand compared to McDonald's, it is definitely positioned as a more Western brand compared to local competitors – and there are plenty of them. The local restaurant chains come in different varieties with different specialties, origins, and size. The biggest local chain, Xiao-Mien-Yang, or Little Lamb, with over 700 restaurants throughout China and even some overseas, originated in Inner Mongolia in 1999 with a specialty for lamb cooked in a "hot pot" with boiling soup similar to Swiss fondue. Another, Zheng-Ding-Ji, specializes in great-tasting boiled chicken with a few dozens of outlets doing excellent business in Shanghai, but it has so far shown little aspiration for any expansion beyond Shanghai. A third, Da-Niang Dumpling, specializes in Chinese-style dumplings with 200 restaurant units in multiple cities. A fourth, Yong He, originated in Taiwan with a specialization in traditional Chinese breakfast – soybean milk and *yiu-tiao*. This chain has also demonstrated a national ambition, especially after its acquisition by Jollibee, a Philippines-based fast-food chain, several years ago. A fifth, Ji Xiang Wanton, has 600 outlets throughout China specializing, as its name indicates, in wanton soup. A sixth, Zheng-Kung-Fu, originated in Guangdong and specializes in steamed soup with Chinese herbal medicinal ingredients, gaining market momentum in a relatively short few years. Interestingly, the local joint venture partner of KFC Shanghai market, New Asia Group, which merged with the Jinjiang Group several years ago, is behind yet another Chinese breakfast-focused fast-food chain, Xin-Ya-Da-Bao, which numbered close to a hundred restaurants in and around Shanghai at one time. None of these local restaurant chains competes directly against KFC. At least, not until KFC introduced *yiu-tiao* at the beginning of 2008.

One chain that does directly compete against KFC is Dicos, based in the city of Tianjin with a few hundred restaurants throughout China, mostly franchised. Started by a Taiwanese company, this fried-chicken-focused restaurant chain has generally stayed away from China's top-tier cities in order to reduce investment and operating expenses, and to avoid head-on competition against KFC. Despite its focus on fried chicken, Dicos poses far less threat to KFC than McDonald's due to relatively inadequate size, geographical coverage, brand recognition, and resource availability.

When positioning against local fast-food chains, KFC relies on its Western roots by building on Chinese consumers' curiosity about the West, scale economy, advertising spending, convenient access to its restaurants at prime locations, and brand leadership. Other factors of differentiation that KFC has depended on in the past include speed and quality of service, operational excellence, freshness of food, interior decor, and cleanliness and orderliness of the dining environment – including the toilet. However, the gap has been narrowing, fast, in recent years.

PROMOTION

Discount-based promotion has long been a common practice within the QSR industry. China is no exception. Between KFC and McDonald's, regardless of which brand initiates a promotion campaign, the other brand almost always responds. In the end, it's not clear if any change in market share or consumer loyalty results from these promotional programs, nor is it clear if either brand's profit margin or, for that matter, total market demand, rises as a result of these discount promotions.

On the other hand, the timing of these promotions can be very intriguing. Toward the end of 2005, while the fear of avian flu was raging across Asia, McDonald's introduced a promotional campaign where on each weekday there was a discounted product package offered. On every Wednesday, for example, a consumer could buy a Big Mac and get a second one free. While there was a tendency for the average Chinese consumer to stay away from chicken products during this period due to a fear of avian flu, it seemed excellent timing to offer brand-neutral QSR fans, or even KFC loyalists, an attractive package of two for the price of one to try Big Macs, a unique product differentiator of McDonald's.

Around the world, McDonald's has been a model for how to successfully market to children. Reflecting the McDonald's heritage of the "Taiwan Gang," KFC China decided early on to focus on children in the development of their advertising and promotional campaigns, borrowing heavily from their McDonald's experience. Eventually, KFC was able to do an even better job than McDonald's in attracting young children to KFC restaurants through the adoption of children-centered initiatives including children's birthday parties, a children's club, children's corners, and children's toys in most KFC restaurants and, above all, through the development and the promotion of "Chicky."

PUBLIC RELATIONS

Ever since KFC China's early days, its public statements have consistently portrayed KFC as a China-friendly company, largely through its workforce and supply chain localization programs. During the second half of the 1990s when business volume began to skyrocket, KFC's Shanghai headquarters had to update its company profile statement every few quarters in terms of the degree of supply localization and the number of local jobs KFC had created in China. By the end of the 1900s, 97 percent of KFC China's food supply originated in China, providing business opportunities to thousands of local companies, giving the vibrant Chinese economy a healthy boost in the arms not just through KFC's direct purchases, but, more importantly, through the economic multiplying effect. At the end of 2007, a little over 2,000 KFC restaurants employed well over 100,000 employees in China. Many hundreds of KFC's direct suppliers and, in turn, many thousands of their suppliers were employing hundreds of thousands more local employees.

KFC has been involved since 1992 with China's most well-known charity, the "Hope Project," which has been focused on children's education in impoverished rural communities throughout China. In 2002, KFC joined hands with China Youth Development Foundation in establishing the KFC China First Light Foundation, which provides scholarships to university students based on need and merit. Many of the scholarship recipients worked for KFC part-time while attending university. Some decided to join KFC full-time upon graduation. Recently, KFC China developed a series of TV commercials highlighting these scholarship recipients. With a few million U.S. dollars of investment, KFC China was able to generate free and complimentary publicity, effective TV advertising, and a reliable source of restaurant management candidates. In Chinese, there has long been a saying, "two birds with a single arrow." In this case, KFC has done even better.

In October 2000, KFC China invited a number of Chinese health experts and government health officials to join the newly established KFC Food Health Consultative Committee. Its stated mission included the introduction of the latest developments in food and nutritional science; to provide KFC with advice and guidance in future development of healthy new products; to provide professional expertise in popularizing public awareness and knowledge of maintaining a healthy and nutritional diet; and to research various projects related to food health. By inviting local Chinese health experts and government officials to become members of this committee, KFC further enhanced its public image as a foreign brand with Chinese characteristics, brought itself closer to local opinion leaders in the food health community, enhanced its legitimacy in handling future crises related to health and food safety through the implicit endorsement of these experts, and solidified its position as the leader of the Chinese food service industry.

In December 2003, KFC China announced the "Health Food Policy White Paper" in an attempt to turn around a rising sentiment against Western fast food based on a growing perception that fast food correlates with obesity, especially children's obesity, and that French fries and other fried and roasted fast-food products are unhealthy food. In the white paper, KFC China pledged its intention to live within the standards set by the Chinese government on all areas of food safety and health; to raise public awareness of nutritional requirements, a balanced diet, and exercise; and to continue the development and introduction of new, diverse, and healthy KFC products to meet the taste preference of Chinese consumers.

In October 2005, KFC China issued a "Proposal for New Fast Food" in which it drew a contrast to traditional Western fast food along the lines of menu choice, local taste, balanced nutrition, cooking method, and food safety. Specifically, the proposal drew public attention to these differences between the "new fast food" and "traditional Western fast food":

First, traditional Western fast food suffers from fixed menus with limited product selections, while the new fast food would continuously develop new product varieties to better accommodate the taste preferences of Chinese consumers.

Second, traditional Western fast food relies on frying as the primary cooking method, resulting in products having a high calorie and fat content. New fast food relies on additional, non-frying cooking methods, including baking ovens, to better match consumer demand for healthy food.

Third, traditional Western fast food is short on vegetables, while the taste is often not acceptable to Chinese consumers. New fast food introduces new vegetable products that better meet Chinese consumers' taste preferences.

Fourth, traditional Western fast food encourages consumers to consume the maximum volume of food. New fast food encourages a balanced diet with moderate volumes.

Fifth, traditional Western fast food applies American food safety management systems wholesale in China. New fast food develops a Chinese-style food safety management system, subjecting all KFC food ingredients to food safety tests conducted in laboratories authorized by the Chinese government.

Sixth, new fast food takes the initiative to communicate with the consuming public about the importance of exercise and maintaining a healthy and balanced diet.

Together, these public announcements made in the years 2000, 2003, and 2005 were designed to forge a favorable public opinion about KFC's commitment to a healthy diet, to fend off criticisms against KFC and other fast-food brands based on health grounds, and to position KFC in the public eye as a socially responsive, caring, and leading advocate for healthier fast food. Once again, KFC was positioned as an industry pioneer and leader. The timing of these public relations events was well planned. It was no accident that they took place during periods of public outcry against fast food and public scares over the consumption of chicken. Together, these programs and actions by KFC China were reminiscent of three of the characteristics of the Chinese martial art of *taiji*, all of which are contrary to the Western way of thinking:

1. React softly to a hard blow when attacked, i.e. "Health Food Policy White Paper"
2. Leverage the force of your opponent in your counterattack, i.e. "KFC Food Health Consultative Committee"
3. Avoid frontal attack through flanking tactics, i.e. "Proposal for New Fast Food"

Only an "intrinsically Chinese" team like KFC's "Taiwan Gang" could have come up with such effective Chinese solutions to Chinese problems.

MEDIA RELATIONS

Factors inherent in the successful management of media relations in China are not much different from those found elsewhere, with one notable exception: government control and influence on the media. To the extent that media relations are still tied to government relations, KFC enjoys a competitive advantage due to its size, its past effort to assist various local Chinese restaurant chains through government-sponsored training programs, and its influence through pseudo-government programs such as the KFC Food Health Consultative Committee. In addition, KFC over the years has conscientiously established and maintained good relations with the domestic food industry, as well as with the general news media at the national level and, in individual KFC markets, at provincial and local levels. Given KFC's size, brand presence, and restaurant industry leadership position, few news media can ignore KFC. This is both a blessing and a curse.

Product and Publicity Risks

Past surveys conducted with Chinese consumers have indicated time and again that although food quality is not the only factor that drives consumer decisions on which fast-food restaurant brand to frequent, it is the most important factor. Among various dimensions for the consideration of food quality, KFC has been a clear winner on variety, frequency, and localization of new products introduced in recent years. On other dimensions of food quality such as consistency and sustainability of consumer preference, however, results to-date are less than clear. For example, two products introduced by KFC at the beginning of 2006, Spicy Diced Chicken and Cod Fillet, were both disappointing. In the former case, it was all bones and little meat. In the latter case, the top and bottom batters combined were thicker than the slice of cod sandwiched in between.

As successful as KFC has been in China, it has yet to learn that it is better not to introduce a new product until it has been fully tested for customer satisfaction. In the long term, it's much better to introduce a richer, more satisfying product at a reduced profit margin than a so-so product backed up with heavy advertising, even if it meets or exceeds internal financial hurdles. Disappointing products create dissatisfied customers who blab to their friends and relatives, creating a vicious cycle of word-of-mouth that can damage future business and, far worse, a brand's reputation.

Sometimes a disappointing product may not be the result of an inadequate or flawed new product development process. Rather, it can be the result of poor execution in a restaurant, such as a deliberate attempt on the part of a restaurant management team to sell products based on ingredients that are no longer fresh.

Although KFC's capability to effectively manage negative publicity has been on the rise since the late 1990s, there has also been a rise in the number and severity of reported incidents adversely affecting KFC's reputation on food quality. In 2005, the "red-dye" incident caught national attention in China for weeks after the news media first reported on March 15 that some KFC products contained the harmful substance Sudan 1 red dye. Later, a supplier admitted fault for having supplied KFC China with food contaminated with red dye. KFC immediately issued a public apology, but the damage was already done.

Responding to public outrage, KFC introduced a number of new measures into its supplier management system, such as introducing new requirements for suppliers to establish internal and external management systems that enable the traceability of raw materials used in the production of KFC products; holding each supplier directly responsible for the quality of its supply chain further upstream; and instituting a system of random safety inspections of each supplier's supply chain.

At about the same time as the red-dye incident, a news report indicated that a KFC restaurant in Hangzhou, Zhejiang Province, had sold products with ingredients past the safety expiration date. Later that year, another report of a similar nature accusing a KFC restaurant of deliberate violation of internal KFC quality standards by selling cooked products beyond the expiration time surfaced in Jingzhou,

Hubei Province. Together, these reports raised the question of how pervasive such practices were within KFC China, thus casting doubt on the company's credibility and reputation.

As the number of KFC restaurants, employees, and new products rise with revenue and profitability, so does the probability for glaring mistakes. When these mistakes do occur, it will be more and more difficult to contain the bad news and control its rippling impact in an age of media explosion.

CONCLUSION

In 1999 ACNielsen conducted a market survey in 30 major cities throughout China. Based on this consumer survey, KFC was ranked "the most frequented international brand" by Chinese consumers, ahead of McDonald's, Coca-Cola, and Nike. Since then, KFC's image as one of the leading foreign brands in China has been further reinforced through significant investments in TV advertising, product promotion, and public relations programs. Together, these programs have been very successful not only in enhancing KFC's brand image, but also in minimizing brand damage in times of adversity.

Unique, good tasting, and innovative products that meet local consumers' preferences have contributed to KFC's enormous success in China. As KFC hastens the pace and variety of new product introductions, it runs the risk of trading speed and variety for food quality. Likewise, as KFC focuses on fast growth, operating efficiency, and profit margin, it runs the risk of sending the wrong signals to its employees at the expense of food and service quality. As KFC's business volume grows, opportunities for mistakes inside KFC restaurants and suppliers' factories may grow proportionally, inevitably attracting negative press attention in a media environment where press freedom has been slowly on the rise.

Therein lies a big and growing challenge for KFC China in the future.

6

SUPPLY CHAIN

INTRODUCTION

On my first day of reporting to work at YUM! Brands Greater China, colleagues from purchasing informed me that each of the KFC markets had their own captive team of buyers. This organizational structure resembled a federation wherein each market was not only a self-contained profit and loss center, but was also in total and full control of its own destiny separate from each other. This had served KFC China's early objective of quickly establishing different market hubs in eastern China as bases for future accelerated growth very well. However, as the number of KFC restaurants multiplied, this highly decentralized organizational structure began to show signs of problems with quality, cost, and operational efficiency.

FROM DECENTRALIZATION TO CENTRALIZATION

What are some of the problem signs? Take supply management or, more specifically, poultry supply management, for instance, which is the most important food category within KFC. Each KFC market had its own group of chicken suppliers, usually from a few to a few dozen depending on the size of the market, preference of the local market management team, supplier availability, and other factors. Some suppliers would supply multiple KFC markets, and get paid different FOB prices for exactly the same chicken product. It got worse than that. At times of a sudden surge in market demand or when supply fell behind demand, different KFC markets would out-bid each other, sometimes creating a self-inflicted run on the market, driving up the price. Occasionally panic would set in, encouraging buying for storage that, in turn, artificially inflated market demand and drove market price further up. Little coordination existed among the different KFC markets. They were, in essence, individual fiefdoms. The purchasing staff in Shanghai headquarters were powerless. At best, this highly decentralized system of procurement presented a classic mathematical dilemma of sub-optimization at the expense of total system optimization. At worst, it represented gross economic inefficiency, internal organizational chaos, and a source of ridicule for suppliers.

It does not take a genius to figure out what needed to be done. Getting it done, however, required a heavy dose of courage, determination, and resolve. Politically, it was a touchy subject because few market general managers and joint venture partners would naturally want to support any move to centralize purchasing, or any other function. But it had to be done, for at least two reasons. The first reason, based on operational quality, cost, and efficiency, was cited in the previous two paragraphs.

The second reason was more strategic in nature. Without a common supply chain and common system standards – especially quality standards – embraced by all KFC markets, any aggressive plan for massive restaurant expansion across China would collapse sooner or later, like building a house on sand. To achieve a single supply chain with a common set of standards to be shared and embraced by all KFC markets meant the days of individual fiefdoms had to end. And so, in 1997, KFC began to consolidate purchasing and QA functions with endorsement from the Executive Committee, composed of Sam Su, president of YUM! Brands Greater China, and most of those who reported directly to Sam, eight all together. New product R&D and distribution/logistics already reported directly into the Shanghai headquarters and would remain that way. Henceforth, all field personnel in these centralized functions would report to a function head based in the Greater China headquarters in Shanghai, not to a market general manager. Even after rounds of discussions and debates with all market general managers in advance, this decision was met with resistance from many of them, as expected. Objections from joint venture partners were even stronger, and persuasion took longer. Eventually all were won over, some reluctantly, by the subsequent business results. People don't like change, especially those changes that take power and authority away from them. Fortunately, you cannot argue with results.

Other functional consolidations soon followed, including IT and real estate development. The Executive Committee decided that market general managers should retain considerable ownership for the growth of their operations through new market development and new restaurant openings, even as they were being asked to focus on restaurant operation. Soon after, support functions such as finance, accounting, HR, and government relations were centralized. Some of these centralized functions, like real estate development, continued to report to market general managers on a dotted-line basis.

This movement toward centralization had to take place in order to prepare KFC China for the next phase of even more aggressive restaurant growth. In 1997, there were over 100 KFC restaurants in 18 KFC markets. Each market contained one or more hub city. By planting a few restaurants on average in each of the top-tier cities, the "hubs," throughout China, KFC had succeeded in laying out an overall structure for future restaurant expansion. The establishment of a distribution center and a delivery network to support all KFC restaurants within a radius of a few hundred kilometers had preceded these "hubs," which was initially an expensive proposition until a critical mass of revenue and profit-generating restaurants had been put in place. This provided yet another economic incentive to implement restaurant expansion with lightning speed. However, before massive restaurant expansion could commence, a common supply chain, restaurant operation, and business management system first had to be put in place in order to ensure uniformly consistent high quality supplies, finished products, and customer services in all KFC markets.

Supply Chain Consolidation

While restaurant expansion continued, a parallel effort to strengthen various support functions and processes through organizational consolidation, system standardization, and employee training and development began. Once again, poultry supply management is a prime example. KFC had a small but strong QA team back in 1997, backed by an effective and comprehensive QA management process called STAR, short for Supplier Tracking Assessment and Recognition. As a QA management system, STAR was equally effective in managing suppliers' factories, third-party warehouses, and KFC restaurants. Unfortunately, the STAR system hadn't been put into full use in China for a variety of reasons, one of which was the decentralized organizational structure that existed up to 1997, making a China-wide program next to impossible to implement. Another reason was that, with this organizational structure, there were too many suppliers, with uneven capabilities, which caused KFC's QA team to be spread too thin to be effective. Supplier consolidation provided the answer to this problem, and more.

To proceed, KFC first invited the heads of different functions, including QA, distribution/logistics, and purchasing, to a meeting with the purpose of determining which poultry suppliers to eliminate, which to keep, and what volume of business to give to each remaining supplier. Lots of "homework" was required before this meeting could take place, however. QA, for example, was asked to present the STAR scores of all KFC poultry suppliers in China for the most recent three years. Distribution/logistics was asked to prepare an assessment of each poultry supplier's warehouse quality, storage capacity, delivery truck capacity and sanitary condition, delivery accuracy, delivery damage and pilferage, employee attitude and responsiveness, record of on-time delivery, and other performance/capability-related evaluation criteria. Purchasing was asked to bring each poultry supplier's production capacity, KFC business volume in recent years, and an assessment of its cost competitiveness and willingness/ability to expand. Then all meeting participants were asked to solicit input in advance from different KFC markets, especially the joint venture markets where resistance to supplier consolidation was strongest. At the meeting it was decided which suppliers to remove, which suppliers to keep, and how much business volume to allocate to each surviving supplier based on an agreed methodology.

In the end, which suppliers to remove turned out to be not as hard a decision as might have been expected. The poultry QA team and poultry purchasing team were both highly regarded in the industry, as was the case with distribution/logistics. With all functional experts gathered in the same room, a supplier's STAR score became the most important determining factor on whether a supplier should stay or be let go. As a result, the number of poultry suppliers was significantly reduced. The remaining suppliers tended to be bigger, more efficient, financially stronger, and more willing and able to invest in new capacity and improved technology to accommodate KFC's projected future business volume.

Next, plans on going forward were communicated to the surviving supplier partners. The importance of certain basic values such as quality, honesty, transparency, fairness, open competition, and delivering commitment were also emphasized. It was made clear to all KFC suppliers that, henceforth, performance results based on STAR, not personal relationships, would become the sole basis of building a mutually supportive and beneficial relationship with KFC. In a society dominated by *guanxi*, this was a new and different approach to supplier relationship management.

After consolidating and restructuring the supplier base, it was time to turn attentions inward once again to focus on redistribution of workloads, re-assignment of supplier responsibility, and internal training and development of QA and purchasing staff, especially those located in different KFC markets away from Shanghai. Regularly scheduled regional meetings and national meetings to communicate, plan, coordinate, and review work progress were held. Training sessions were held back-to-back with these meetings to save travel time and expense. Senior mangement attended these meetings as much as their schedules allowed to show support for the respective functional leaders, and to explain the new organizational structure, the importance of STAR, the new way of interacting with suppliers, and to respond to employees' questions in person. To facilitate inter-office communication and to promote employee career development, staff from Shanghai headquarters were transferred to different KFC markets, and vice versa, often for months at a time.

Not surprisingly, KFC China's cost of sourcing chicken dropped significantly while the quality of chicken sourced rose noticeably, thanks to supplier consolidation and continuing, rigorous enforcement of STAR by both QA and purchasing. By significantly reducing the number of poultry suppliers, the remaining suppliers on average received bigger purchase volumes and a stronger assurance of order stability from KFC, allowing them to take the necessary actions to further reduce cost, expand production capacity, and use KFC as a reference account to generate new customers and new business volume, all of which made them more productive, cost-efficient, and competitive. Of course, some of those cost savings were passed on to KFC.

By having the same number of KFC QA and purchasing staff working with far fewer suppliers, each supplier was able to get far more time, attention, and support from KFC. KFC, in turn, benefited from higher-quality raw materials, at reduced purchase prices and transaction costs. Similar consolidation of suppliers expanded to cover all external purchases – food items such as buns, salad, and dressings, as well as non-food items such as papers, cups, disposable forks, knives, tea spoons, menu boards, toy equipment, construction equipment, and furniture.

Supply Localization

In addition to the consolidation of suppliers, KFC also initiated a program to speed up the local sourcing of all supplies, beginning with the big-ticket items and big-volume items such as menu boards, refrigerators, freezers, stainless fabricated kitchen equipment, toy equipment, and the remaining imported food items such as sauces and spices, ice tea, and hot chocolate. Together, these items generated maximum savings. Soon there remained only a few major imported food items including the KFC Original Recipe mix, which was produced by one global supplier in order to protect this critical trade secret, plus French fries and cobbed corns because few of the locally-grown-and-harvested crops had met KFC's product specification after years of cultivation by local growers.

Savings resulting from supply chain consolidation and supply localization alone during 1998 amounted to over US$10 million. Cost of goods sold in an average KFC restaurant declined from 42 to 39 percent during 1998, even in the face of higher-than-normal product discounts in response to business slowdown due to the Asian financial crisis. During 1999, KFC China's cost of goods sold continued to decline, but the most important payoff from these internal and external actions lay in the creation of a new supply chain system based on which an aggressive, and orderly, restaurant expansion drive in the ensuing years became feasible.

Competitive Bidding

During 2000, in a continuous drive to reduce the cost of goods sold and to prevent possible collusion between members of KFC's purchasing staff and suppliers, KFC China introduced a supplier bidding process. The original design called for an open, fair, and competitive bidding process to take place every six months in order to stimulate actions of continuous improvement on the part of KFC suppliers. To reduce the risk of supply disruption, a minimum of two suppliers for each stock keeping unit (SKU) was preferred. In select cases where a single supplier was unavoidable, analytical tools such as cost bar analysis and industry benchmarking were adopted. In all other cases, a bidding process was put in place. This open bidding process was a tough, competitive, and demanding process for KFC's suppliers, representing a new way of doing business with KFC based on price, cost, and product quality.

The outcome of each round of bidding was the allocation of KFC's estimated demand volume for the coming six months among all qualified suppliers. During each new round of bidding, following the order of bidding price from the lowest (X) to the highest, each qualified supplier (Y) was asked to match the price of X in order to protect Y's existing volume of purchase by KFC. If Y agreed to match the price of X, his purchase volume was protected for the next six months. If Y refused to match the price of X, Y's volume was then awarded to X unless X's maximum production capacity or KFC's internal guideline threshold to avoid single-supplier risk was reached. Six months later, this bidding process repeated itself.

The adoption of this open bidding process helped KFC China in the continuous reduction of its cost of goods sold, from 38 percent of revenues in 2003 to 37 percent in 2004, and 36 percent in 2005.

Assuming total annual revenue of US$1 billion, each percentage drop in the cost of goods sold translated into US$10 million of cost savings or, putting it another way, US$10 million of additional profit each year, year after year.

Supplier Interactions

I've lost count of how many chicken farms and processing plants I visited during those years, even as I dreaded the sight, the sound, and the smell of chickens being raised and slaughtered. We wanted the key suppliers to know that KFC cared about them. Suppliers are critical to KFC's success. Frequent contact with key suppliers encourages better understanding and more effective work relationships. Once I was able to persuade myself to repeatedly visit the chicken farms and the slaughter houses, the rest of my supplier visits to bread factories, ice cream factories, salad processing factories, even kitchen equipment and menu board factories, suddenly became so much more enjoyable.

A common complaint from suppliers and employees alike is that it is a tough and demanding experience to be a supplier to KFC China. That's the way it ought to be. In business, as in life, great achievement demands extraordinary efforts and, sometimes, great sacrifices. Fortunately, in the case of KFC China, these efforts did not go to waste. Over the years, many of KFC's suppliers have become the leaders of their respective industries. Some have built sizeable companies with KFC's business volume at their core; others have expanded to new markets across China, sometimes beyond China, based on KFC's reputation for demanding the highest quality at a competitive cost from all suppliers.

While the QA and purchasing teams were busy consolidating local suppliers of product categories such as poultry in which KFC China had an excess of suppliers, at the same time KFC was also busy bringing on board new suppliers. These new suppliers were intended to achieve three different objectives. First, to upgrade the quality of the supply chain by replacing poor performing suppliers. Second, to minimize supply interruption risk by avoiding single-source supply categories. Third, to increase locally produced products and services by convincing foreign suppliers to set up and expand their local production capacity in China, and by sourcing from qualified local Chinese suppliers. The amount of work required of our QA and purchasing teams before a new supplier was certified under the STAR system was enormous, but such resource investment was necessary for the long-term benefit of KFC China.

At the end of 1999, I led a small group of KFC China's largest poultry suppliers on a tour of American poultry farms and processing plants. It was in response to a long-standing request from many of KFC China's poultry suppliers. At long last, KFC was able to respond to their repeated requests, as a service and a reward to these supplier partners. On this trip through America's Deep South, these suppliers learned by observing what the world's most technically advanced nation is doing in an industry with which they are very familiar, and assessing how much of what they observed could be applied back home. Needless to say, this trip also opened a few doors across the Pacific, which led to a few additional import/export and joint venture agreements.

Opportunities for cooperation were ample. Those U.S. poultry suppliers interested in penetrating the China market were able to exchange technology for market access. Those who were not interested in setting up direct operations in China could export chicken wings, feet, necks, innards, and other parts of a chicken not desired by American consumers, but craved by their Chinese counterparts, to China. Likewise, Chinese poultry processors could export white breast meat to America. Assuming minimum import duties and cost of freight and insurance, both American and Chinese producers are able to export for more attractive prices than those obtainable in their respective home markets due to the complementary nature of supply and demand curves for the same part of a chicken in two different markets. Such exchange makes good economic sense not only between China and the U.S., but also when expanded to incorporate other top poultry-producing countries both in Asia (such as Thailand) and further afield (such as Brazil).

DISTRIBUTION AND LOGISTICS

At the beginning of 2008, KFC had slightly over 2,000 restaurants throughout China, compared to McDonald's with less than half that number. At the turn of the century, they were neck-to-neck. What happened? What contributed to McDonald's less-than-satisfying business performance in China? It's a complex, and important, question to raise, one that has been partially explored in Chapters 2 through 5 of this book beginning with the assembly of a leadership team. But distribution and logistics have also contributed to the widening gap in size, profitability, and speed of restaurant expansion between KFC and McDonald's.

I toured a McDonald's warehouse in the suburbs of Shanghai after leaving KFC. It was a green-field warehouse – a very modern, impressive facility located inside an industrial park with space for future expansion. Inside the warehouse, it was divided into different sections, each with different interior temperature levels from room temperature to frozen storage, automatic loading equipment, and a fully computerized inventory management system. Outside the warehouse, a huge 18-wheel delivery truck was waiting on the loading dock, getting ready for the next delivery shipment to various McDonald's restaurants in nearby cities. I was awe-struck by this modern facility, one of the best-equipped warehouses I have seen anywhere – and I've seen quite a few. If the Chinese characters on the front gate and on the side of the truck had been replaced with English, the same physical assets could have been airlifted to somewhere in the middle of Iowa USA and would have fit right in. Trouble is, this warehouse is located in China. I don't mean to imply that these physical assets have been misplaced in China. I do, however, question their timing.

At the same time, KFC China was, in fact, planning to upgrade its own logistics and distribution facilities in China, but was several years behind McDonald's in its implementation, by design. Why? The economic justification wasn't there, nor was China's road infrastructure ready to support investment in an 18-wheel trailer. While no expressway existed anywhere in China throughout the 1980s, construction of expressways began in the 1990s, and has been going non-stop ever since. By 2007, China's expressway system has multiplied severalfold compared to the beginning of this century, linking all big cities and many medium-sized cities throughout China, thus making an 18-wheeler a practical financial investment. But such wasn't the case in 2000.

Another example that casts doubt on McDonald's cost competitiveness is the new and automated warehouse I toured with advanced material handling, temperature control, and computing equipment imported from the U.S. By building an automated facility in a business environment where revenue has been growing slower than planned and where the cost of labor is relatively low, I suspect both McDonald's and its third-party logistics partner must have been under heavy cost pressure at the time of my visit, possibly continuing to the present if it remains an operation dedicated to serving McDonald's, and McDonald's alone.

By comparison, KFC's distribution and logistics operation in China is a captive operation directly owned and managed by KFC. Its sole mission is to support KFC restaurants and KFC's strategy of rapid restaurant expansion. For years, KFC China leased existing warehouse facilities, upgraded the physical facilities to meet KFC's internal health and safety standards based on the STAR system, staffed these warehouses with trained KFC employees, and managed the people and the facilities directly and actively. Because its distribution and logistics operation had been a captive operation from day one, KFC China never had to worry about strategic partners' profit margins, readiness and desire to expand, inter-company communication and coordination, etc. Instead, once a decision is made to enter a new province, a new city, or a new township, KFC's captive logistics and distribution team simply goes to work – quickly and efficiently.

The work may require KFC's trucking fleet to climb mountains thousands of feet high, or cross waters hundreds of feet deep, but the general attitude long-held within this team has been: we are here to serve the needs of KFC restaurants, come hell or high water. This somewhat extreme service attitude comes directly from the leader of this team, Ray Tian, another member of the "Taiwan Gang." I remember riding from KFC's Guangzhou distribution center to Haikou, Hainan Island, as part of a routing and site investigation journey shortly before a decision was made for KFC to open the first KFC restaurant on Hainan Island. The ride took over ten hours, including the time to cross the Qiongzhou Strait on a ferry, the first time for a KFC delivery truck. It wouldn't be the last.

During my tenure I visited every single KFC warehouse in China, some more than a few times. KFC employees manning these warehouses and driving those delivery trucks, usually late at night on roadways that are not well-lit and often under extremely hazardous road conditions, are the unsung heroes of KFC China. They deserve to be recognized and praised, again and again.

Distribution/logistics is one of the most important competitive differentiators enjoyed by KFC China. With distribution and logistics resources completely and directly under its own control, KFC has been able to go further and faster into the Chinese inland in an attempt to aggressively expand its market reach, and to do so far more efficiently and cost-effectively than the competition. It is a complementary, and necessary, ingredient for the successful execution of KFC's strategy of rapid and profitable restaurant growth. Without it, the strategy could not possibly have been put into practice.

Ironically, at one point in time this view was not widely shared within the leadership team of KFC China nor, for that matter, within YUM! Brands. In fact, I still remember responding to a query about when KFC China would spin off this part of its operation during my very first presentation to Andy Pearson and David Novak, who were then, respectively, the CEO and the COO of YUM! Brands. During the rest of my career at KFC, each year I had to deal with reminders from various sources that YUM! Brands prefers not to own and operate its own distribution and logistics network anywhere around the world.

CORRUPTION

Perhaps the most painful of my China business experiences is related to questionable, or outright corrupt, business practices. In 1995, I resigned from a Fortune 500 company as the general manager of north Asia, in part because I was the lone holdout in its Asia headquarters against signing a joint venture agreement – an agreement that I had personally negotiated with a provincial telecommunications bureau in China. Within sight of signing, my negotiation counterpart demanded a commission based on a fixed percentage of the value of all imported sub-assembly of electronic parts to be passed through a designated import-export company. My two colleagues at the time, the head of Asia finance and the head of Asia legal, kept on assuring me that it was a common practice. By remaining silent on the issue, my boss, the head of Asia, was sending me what I thought to be clear signals. After all, here is someone being groomed to become the next corporate CFO, and needing to show business results in his first line assignment. To this day, I still don't know for sure if it's legal or not, but I did feel then, as I do now, that it was an ethically questionable practice. After losing many nights of sleep over it, in the end another innocuous incident gave me the excuse to leave the company.

Winding the clock forward to 2001, I left KFC to take on a new career challenge as the chief operating officer of a trouble-ridden, China-based, U.S.-venture-capital-funded, Internet portal startup. It's amazing how many business problems a young company of a little over a year old is able to accumulate, but those business problems did not faze me – on the contrary, they were the exact reasons that attracted me to leave the relative comfort of KFC to take on a young, small, and troubling startup. In the process of fixing legacy problems, I discovered that this company had been paying employees of client companies kickbacks, authorized by one of the two founders. I approached the founder, and his view was "why can't we do this if it's a common practice in China?" I don't know how common such practices are in China, and to be honest, I am afraid to find out, but I knew right there and then that I had to go. Later, after fixing all of the legacy problems, I turned in my resignation to the board of directors.

Twice in the past decade I have left otherwise challenging, interesting, and rewarding careers due to questionable business practices. Both events took place in China. Because of events like these, I was very careful during my career with KFC when it came to dealing with suppliers. While mindful of the official company policy and guidelines, I followed my own personal rules, which went even further: No joint entertainment of any kind with suppliers, except at official company events such as annual company gala dinners. Accept no gift of any kind, large or small. All meetings will be conducted inside an office. No business meals with suppliers unless paid for by KFC, except when I am a guest while visiting a supplier's factory and so on.

Examples abound: I remember one supplier who left a box of four traditional Chinese moon cakes normally consumed during the Mid-Autumn (Moon) Festival on the desk of my assistant. After returning to my office from an out-of-town trip, I asked my assistant to please return the moon cakes with a polite letter thanking the supplier and explaining the reasons why I could not accept any gift, large or small, from any KFC supplier. Some of my closest colleagues, including those from purchasing, criticized me for being too strict, behaving in a way devoid of the human touch. Reflecting back today, I can't say they were wrong. I can say, however, that as strict as my own personal rules and behavior were, they did not stop at least two KFC employees from accepting kickbacks from suppliers. I sacked both of them. I can forgive business mistakes, even failures, but I can't forgive outright lies and corrupt practices.

An effective leader practices what he or she believes and preaches. Lead through example. Walk the talk. Due to the sensitivity of the functions I oversaw at KFC China, many of which dealt on a daily basis with suppliers, I was particularly careful in living a strict personal code of conduct every day to set a good example for all employees to see. In addition, KFC had all the preventive systems available to big multinational corporations put in place, from new employee reference checking to business ethics training. In the end, we were unable to prevent those two KFC employees from misconduct of a most serious nature. What went wrong? What more could I, as their leader, have done in order to prevent such employee misconduct? In the past few years I have come to this conclusion: very little. This conclusion is based on the observation that corruption is not simply a business problem, it's a societal problem. Pervasive corrupt practices reflect society at large. This may sound like a harsh statement, but it's true. The evidence supporting it doesn't just stop with the examples above. In the past few years, it's been difficult in China to flip open a daily newspaper without a reference to corruption.

Why is Corruption so Widespread

But why is corruption so widespread – some might even say rampant – in China? Ironically, part of the answer lies in China's economic reforms. Once the economic reforms took a turn from socialist idealism to a market economy, private ownership, and the accumulation of wealth, personal financial interests became an overriding consideration in a society short on spiritual and moral guidance and increasingly bent on material pursuits. In a way, the economic opening of China inevitably led to corrupt practices in the absence of any formal, structured ethical framework, nor any moral compass of substance. In the past, China was not like this.

For over 2,000 years, in the absence of an official religion, Confucianism, Taoism, and Buddhism together formed the basis of moral conduct for the average Chinese citizen. Concepts such as *Li* (civility), *Yi* (loyalty, obligations), *Lian* (integrity, incorruptness), and *Chi* (shame) have served as moral and behavioral guidelines for centuries. Many of these traditional values came under attack during the first fifty years of rule by the CCP, culminating in the catastrophic decade of the Cultural Revolution, during which many of China's traditional values were trampled on under the guise of "smashing Confucianism."

During the first three decades of communist rule, traditional Chinese values were replaced by altruistic, socialist values advocating economic equality, selflessness, and public service. Private property was confiscated, removing almost all private and individual economic incentives. With the arrival of economic reforms, China was left without traditional Chinese ethics, nor socialist idealism. Since religion never took root in China during the past 2,000 years, the net result is an absence of any structured social moral compass since the start of China's economic reforms in 1978.

Fortunately, China's top leadership is aware of the dangers that lie ahead, and has taken active steps since the beginning of this century to revive the study of Confucianism, even encouraging religious practices as long as they do not threaten communist rule in China.

Roots of Corruption: Civil Service and A Culture of *Guanxi*

The roots of corruption in China can be traced as far back as the Han Dynasty (206 BC – 220 AD), when Confucianism was first established as the official state philosophy, with emphasis on the absolute authority of the emperor and the hierarchical order of traditional Chinese society. Later, during the early seventh century, a civil service system was established based on a series of state-sponsored written examinations grounded in the Confucian classics. Scoring high on a progressive series of examinations was the prerequisite to government posts, social status, fame, and for some, fortune through corruption. This is why advanced education has been highly sought after by Chinese for over a thousand years. Of course, not all government bureaucrats are corrupt, and some dynasties have been more corrupt than others. Corruption usually rises as a dynasty enters its declining phase. For example, during the second half of the last Chinese dynasty, the Qing, official titles and government posts could be purchased by wealthy landowners and merchants otherwise unable to qualify under the civil examination system. Needless to say, many buyers expected a healthy return on their financial investment, and the imperial court was well aware of this, which made the situation tantamount to corruption blessed by the state.

The Chinese concept of *guanxi* also helps encourage corrupt practices. What is *guanxi*? A simple explanation of the word is inter-personal relationships or connections. Between two individuals, *guanxi* can be initiated based on some common, or shared, characteristics – family name and origin, place of birth, school, work, common friend, or acquaintance. Once *guanxi* is initiated and established, trust, affinity, and a sense of obligation can be developed over time, based on which personal favors can be asked of each other. To put it bluntly, in the worst case, *guanxi*-building is a courting process aimed at mutual support and benefit, a process of exchange and trading favors – "I scratch your back, and you scratch mine."

Ultimately, *guanxi* is a system based on individuals and relationships between them, not on law. This man-centered element of Confucianism manifests itself in all aspects of Chinese society. In business and government, it often blurs the dividing line between what are private interests versus what are public interests; what is a personal relationship versus what is publicly accountable. Thus, a company's general manager is inclined to provide special favors to friends and relatives in recruiting, promoting, reprimanding, and other forms of reward and punishment. In politics, it works in a similar way. One of the clearest manifestations of *guanxi* in modern China is the so-called "Gang of the Princes," wherein many of China's rising political and business leaders are sons and daughters of the first and second-generation leaders of the CCP. What is the difference between "favoritism" and "corruption"? It is unclear, but whatever it is, the line between them must not be too thick.

Future of Corruption

Will corruption in China get any worse before it gets better? It's hard to say. However, we know that the problem has seriously eroded public trust during the years of China's economic reforms, and has increasingly been viewed by the top CCP leadership as one of the most serious challenges it faces in the years ahead. In a recent report released by the CCP, over 115,000 party members were punished after investigations of various charges during 2005. Although the charges were not broken down by categories, we can assume that a good portion, if not an overwhelming majority, of them were related to corruption, including six cases involving the highest administrative positions in the Chinese government such as the head or deputy head of a central government ministry, or the head or deputy head of a province.

During 2006, corruption scandals rose to a new height, capped by the arrest of Chen Liang-Yu, CCP boss of Shanghai, a member of the Politburo, and protégé of Jiang Ze-Min, the former paramount leader of China. On April 11, 2008, after a long delay, Chen Liang-Yu was sentenced to 18 years in prison. To conclude with the statement that corruption reaches the highest levels within the CCP is not an exaggeration. As many as 4,000 government officials have pocketed more than US$50 billion and fled the country in recent years, according to one Chinese news source.

These statistics indicate both the widespread nature of corruption among CCP members and government officials – who are the political, economic, and social elite of China today – as well as the CCP's determination to eradicate them. Yet, despite strong measures taken to punish corrupt officials in recent years, corruption continues. This does not seem to lend an optimistic assessment for the future. However, to conclude that corruption is deeply rooted in the Chinese culture and, therefore, is difficult if not impossible to eradicate seems premature in view of the achievements of both Hong Kong and Singapore in recent decades. Their lessons seem to indicate that the right systems put in place will change people's behavior, if not values, over time. But any improvement may take generations, and will require heavy doses of both courage and resolve from the highest levels of China's political leadership.

CONCLUSION

In some manufacturing and retail companies around the world, distribution and logistics are often viewed as non-core competencies. In developed countries, most QSR companies, KFC included, outsource their logistics and distribution functions to third parties. In China this option of outsourcing did not exist back in the 1980s and 1990s. Even at the beginning of the new century, it was not easy to find world-class, third-party logistics companies with a network of multi-temperature warehouses and trucking fleets operating in multiple regions throughout China.

KFC and McDonald's faced exactly the same set of market conditions at their respective entry into China, but each came up with very different solutions, reflecting perhaps their respective "corporate gene." In essence, McDonald's went the way of outsourcing and decided to import its solution through a third-party strategic partner based in the U.S. KFC, on the other hand, decided to develop, from scratch, a local solution based on captive ownership and direct management.

KFC built and controlled its own logistics and warehousing capabilities from the very beginning, often by leveraging existing physical infrastructure of its local joint venture partners, and introducing KFC management systems and management personnel trained by KFC. By insisting on direct company control and refining existing infrastructure through "software" upgrades instead of expensive capital investment in "hardware" upgrades, KFC's logistics and warehousing system supported and enabled KFC China's strategy of rapid restaurant expansion to the remotest corners of China at relatively low cost, high efficiency and speed, generating sustainable competitive cost and other strategic advantages for KFC in the process.

REAL ESTATE DEVELOPMENT

INTRODUCTION

Officially, my first day at work was Monday, October 6, 1997. Unofficially, the first KFC meeting I attended took place on Friday of the prior week. It was a real estate development meeting. In the QSR industry, real estate development means the planning, site selection, lease negotiation and renewal, construction, and maintenance of new and existing restaurants.

In the subsequent three-plus years, I co-chaired many dozens of such meetings, during which every single proposal for a new KFC and Pizza Hut restaurant within Greater China was reviewed and approved (or rejected). No month went by without at least one such meeting, each requiring at least half a day. Prior to each meeting, much work had already gone into the preparation for each proposed new restaurant site, involving hundreds, sometimes thousands, of man-hours of team effort. Over the years, KFC China has consistently invested heavy resources into the real estate development function, as do all industry players around the world, for good business reasons. Simply put, in the QSR industry, site selection is a key success factor. Some industry experts would say it's the most critical, certainly the most visible, of all industry key success factors.

Real estate development is a key driver for a fast-food restaurant chain's success. In the case of KFC China, it is also the function that underpins the company's fundamental business strategy, which is to rapidly accumulate scale through restaurant expansion. Given this strategy, over the years KFC has often been the first Western restaurant brand to enter a small or medium-sized Chinese city or township. This reputation as the industry pioneer has followed KFC everywhere in China since its market entry in 1987, but especially since the mid-1990s.

While seemingly risky, this pioneering strategy has served KFC China very well in both the short and the long term. In the short term, the first few KFC restaurants in a new city tend to enjoy higher levels of profit compared to those opening later. In the long term, KFC has been able to build a strong growth momentum, brand recognition, and economies of scale through a continuing stream of new restaurants.

MARKET PLANNING AND SITE SELECTION

Planning for new market entry, be it a province, a city, or a township, can take years, as is the case with targeting specific restaurant locations in any given city. Relationships with owners of buildings at prime locations need to be developed, and maintained, for years before they bear fruit. Likewise, relationships with government officials at various levels in new cities, counties, and townships need to be developed and maintained for years before the first KFC restaurant opens for business. Often, the local government is KFC's regulator, license approver, landlord, and customer.

Restaurant site selection is a relatively mature business discipline in developed countries, with forecasting models backed up by years of fact-based validation. In China, the same forecasting models had to undergo major refinements and modifications in order to better accommodate much greater pedestrian and bicycle traffic volume; much more rapid changes in urban land development, zoning, and re-zoning; and time-compressed, often generation-skipping, rapid change in the local retailing scene.

KFC is usually able to obtain attractive lease and payment terms from a landlord because of its size and brand image. On lease term, eight years or more compared to the usual two to four years for an average retail tenant. On payment terms, many landlords can be convinced to accept a fixed percentage of a KFC restaurant's monthly revenue, which is often preferred by KFC in order to reduce financial risks associated with the uncertainty of a restaurant's future revenue stream, especially prior to its grand opening. As the biggest restaurant chain in China, KFC is usually the most preferred tenant among all QSR brands. In an industry where a restaurant's location is a key success factor, KFC's brand reputation provides yet another important leverage point in order to obtain the most attractive locations at the lowest rental cost, further propagating the self-fulfilling prophecy of being China's number one restaurant brand.

Co-branding

This benevolent cycle manifests itself in other ways, one of which is through co-branding, both internal and external. External co-branding means co-habiting, or sharing a common site, with big name retailers – oftentimes hypermarket operators such as Carrefour and Wal-Mart. Being the number one restaurant chain in China, KFC is one of the most preferred tenants for these hypermarket operators, which usually serve as both the property manager and the anchor tenant for a new shopping center. Most of these hypermarket projects prefer a fast-food restaurant located in the shopping center. YUM! Brands had initiated negotiations with Carrefour for an agreement giving KFC first right-of-refusal in future Carrefour projects. Carrefour was our first choice because the French retailer, like KFC, was an early entrant into China and has become the most successful operator in China's hypermarket industry. Carrefour China's general manager once told me that a cooperative agreement between Carrefour and KFC is a perfect match between two leading brands in their respective industries. For KFC, it's another example of success begetting more success.

Internal co-branding is a unique advantage KFC enjoys over its competitors worldwide. In addition to KFC, YUM! Brands has so far introduced into China: Pizza Hut, Pizza Hut Express (home delivery service), Taco Bell (which pulled out in 2007), and East Dawning.

Of these, KFC and Pizza Hut are the only brands that have achieved financial success and brand recognition so far. Already, co-habitation of KFC and Pizza Hut in the same shopping mall or even adjacent to each other can be found in Shanghai and other cities. As YUM! Brands gears up East Dawning and other brands for launch and expansion in the years ahead, internal co-branding will rise in its economic and marketing significance.

RESTAURANT DESIGN AND CONSTRUCTION

Not all tasks related to real estate development and life cycle management are handled by KFC employees. While market planning, site selection, and lease negotiation are tasks handled by KFC personnel, restaurant design, construction and lifecycle maintenance are outsourced. What's involved in these outsourced tasks is often tedious but necessary, and not without its own challenges.

Prior to 2000, almost all of KFC China's restaurant design jobs were put out to design firms based in Taiwan. These are architectural design firms that came to China at the invitation of KFC back in the 1980s and early 1990s because they were already familiar with the various internal KFC restaurant design specifications and standards in Taiwan and, therefore, required little coaching. As KFC expanded throughout China, these architectural design firms followed KFC every step of the way. As a result, despite the fact that KFC restaurants in China come in different sizes and shapes, all of them look and feel the same to KFC customers regardless of location. The fact that this has been achieved in the face of multiple interior and exterior design models and specifications introduced by KFC in a period of rapid restaurant expansion, often with a tight demand on schedule, should not be taken for granted.

In a way, these different KFC designs for restaurant interiors and exteriors represent another level of "localization" in which different restaurant size, location, and target customer segments result in the adoption of different design models for a given KFC restaurant. For example, a KFC restaurant located in a residential community with children being a key target customer segment would most likely have in its design a "kids' corner" in the restaurant's dining area to be used for birthday parties and other kids-oriented programs and activities, and a kids' play area with children's toys such as slides. Another KFC restaurant located in a big city's office district would have a modern design with more metals and soothing colors.

In the race to open the next new KFC restaurant, one of the biggest challenges is on-time delivery, with all of the finishing touches, down to the garbage cans and washroom detergent dispensers. When required, a new KFC restaurant can be made ready for its grand opening within a month after a rental lease agreement for the restaurant property has been signed. It's all part of the service attitude referred to earlier and a company-wide focus on speed, which permeates throughout KFC China and its supply chain, from architectural design firms to construction contractors.

Restaurant Design Localization

Compared with an average KFC restaurant in the U.S., the average KFC restaurant in China differs in at least three major ways. First, the average daily customer count and transaction volumes are much larger. Second, although more restaurant take-outs can be found in China today compared to five or ten years ago, especially in big cities, KFC remains largely a sit-down dining experience. Third, despite rapid growth in private automobile ownership since 2000, drive-through remains an insignificant development so far due to city planning restrictions as well as a shortage of market demand. In fact, after launching its very first drive-through restaurant in 2002 in Beijing, KFC only launched the second one three years later in Shanghai. In 2006, senior members of the McDonald's China leadership team made a number of press announcements touting the strategic importance of drive-through restaurants to the future of McDonald's China. They may be disappointed if the future focus is on drive-through restaurants in the inner cities. However, the fate of drive-through restaurants could be very different along China's multiplying expressways.

These three differences in market characteristics require very different restaurant design and layout for an average KFC restaurant in China compared to the U.S. First of all, the average restaurant in China has a much larger dining area, with an average of 200–300 seats per restaurant. Second, the amount of frying equipment in the kitchen is greater, given China's much bigger transaction volume per restaurant, which together with in-restaurant storage results in bigger space requirements for kitchen and storage. Third, the volume of equipment required behind the counter also multiplies as a result of the bigger transaction volume. For example, while the average KFC restaurant in the U.S. may have three or four cash registers, it's not unusual to see seven, eight, or many more in China. Fourth, due to high traffic volumes, especially at peak times during an average day, the area in front of the counter in China is much bigger than what would be typically found in the U.S. in order to avoid queues lining up outside a restaurant, which still happens from time to time in China, especially during the initial weeks after the first KFC restaurant's grand opening in a new town. Fifth, there is obviously no need for any drive-through windows or associated equipment and space for most KFC restaurants in the foreseeable future.

Once again, unique market characteristics found in China required flexibility in making timely and appropriate adjustments to restaurant design by KFC China's local team and suppliers, with strong support and timely approval from headquarters in the U.S.

Beijing Heroes

In 1997, there was a significant gap in the number of restaurants between KFC and McDonald's in Beijing, with KFC trailing. This was largely a result of KFC joint venture partners' lack of interest in the continuing investment required of rapid restaurant expansion. With KFC leading most markets in China, KFC Beijing had long been an internal embarrassment. After all, Beijing is not only the nation's capital, it's also where the first KFC restaurant was planted in 1987 – the birthplace of KFC China. To be the leading restaurant brand in China and yet to trail behind McDonald's in the nation's capital and KFC's birthplace was simply too glaring an irony to be ignored.

Consequently, there was a determined effort to change that. The job became easier after the local joint venture partners fell in line to support an accelerated restaurant growth plan. KFC began to build and develop a real estate development team in Beijing headed by Zheng Gang, a smart and determined young man who is a law graduate of

Beijing University, sometimes known within academic circles as "the Harvard of China," while known by most Chinese simply as Bei-Da. Zheng Gang did not have any QSR industry experience or, for that matter, any experience identifying successful retail sites. But he had high personal integrity and was smart, driven, outspoken, daring, willing to learn, and hard working.

In the ensuing few years, KFC Shanghai Restaurant Support Center trained, assisted, challenged, and cheered Zheng Gang and his real estate development team as progress was made each year to edge closer to McDonald's in the Beijing market. During those years, every time I was in Beijing I would try to "sweep the streets" with him or members of his team to get a first-hand view of the potential restaurant sites and to see if they needed additional help or support from Shanghai. In 2002, KFC Beijing finally succeeded in retaking the market leadership position not only in sales revenue, but also in number of restaurants.

LOCATION, LOCATION, LOCATION

Of all forms of advertising and promotion, none is more effective for the purpose of branding than KFC restaurants placed at strategic locations. First, the convenience factor; if a KFC restaurant can be found at every corner where crowds gather, customers will come because it's convenient. Second, the name factor; if the fact that KFC is the number one restaurant brand in China is widely known or, better yet, widely seen, Chinese consumers will come because of its industry leadership position. The omnipresence of KFC restaurants reinforces the brand image of being number one. Third, the herd instinct; Chinese consumers are used to crowds and many are attracted by, and drawn to, crowds. A KFC restaurant located at a busy intersection crowded with customers will attract even more customers. Fourth, while advertising promotes brand and product awareness, a customer's positive experience inside one or more KFC restaurants reinforces a favorable brand image even more, much more in fact.

On the other hand, a poorly performing restaurant can be a big pain. Not only because each new restaurant on average requires approximately half a million U.S. dollars of cash investment, but also because the operating loss from a single under-performing restaurant can easily offset healthy profits generated from several profitable ones. Therefore, while maximizing each new restaurant's profit is important, so is the avoidance of poorly performing ones. Is there a foolproof way to achieve both? Sadly not, but what can be achieved is an attempt to maximize the probability of success and, at the same time, minimize the likelihood of failure – especially major catastrophes – through systems, procedures, accumulation of experience, and improved judgment over time.

At KFC China, a system for evaluating each proposed new restaurant location has been evolving for years. While lots of different data are collected for each proposed site ranging from economic statistics to traffic count, the final decision of "go" or "no go" for a proposed new restaurant site is not based on any fixed formula whereby a built-in mathematical algorithm would automatically spell out an answer. Instead, the go/no-go decision is the result of a combination of data analysis and human judgment, following a well-refined process.

Before a lease agreement for a new restaurant site is signed, three levels of approval are necessary. First, at each KFC market where a proposed site originates, a real estate committee, usually made up of the market general manager and the function heads for real estate development, restaurant operation, and finance, must sign off on the proposed site. Once approved by the market real estate committee, a proposal then goes to the Shanghai Restaurant Support Center's real estate committee, which in the late 1990s was composed of three vice presidents – restaurant operation, finance, and business development. Depending on the volume of new proposals, this committee meets monthly, bi-weekly, or even weekly. Decisions are made swiftly, most of the time. Most proposals receive a yes or no decision on the spot. Some require additional data, usually because the merit of their approval is being questioned. These real estate committee meetings take up a lot of the KFC China leadership team's time and effort – valuable company resources. Behind the scenes, even more, much more, time and effort go into the preparation for each new restaurant proposal. These collective efforts are not only necessary, but also well worthwhile. Better to spend time and effort upfront in order to prevent a disaster in the making than to spend time and effort cleaning up after one. The third level of approval takes place in Dallas, Texas, where the YUM! Brands international division is headquartered. However, this is mostly a formality.

Cleaning Up Disasters

Even after all this time and effort spent on inspecting, analyzing, discussing, and evaluating each newly proposed restaurant site, KFC China was not free from problem restaurants. After the Asian financial crisis hit in 1997, business suffered and revenue per KFC restaurant spiraled downward. While a rising tide carries all ships, an ebbing tide exposes the weak. And an ebbing tide it was. The real estate committee began developing a rescue mission plan after first identifying and categorizing all problem restaurants. One by one, we analyzed the facts and the data surrounding each problem restaurant, developed separate and individual rescue plans, executed, and kept a watchful eye for signs of recovery. In a few cases we decided to shut them down, taking the losses in one gulp instead of dying slow, painful deaths.

A lot was learned from that exercise. On negotiating lease agreements, for example, KFC learned the importance of insisting on an escape clause in every single lease agreement, regardless of how promising a proposed site may appear. KFC also learned the desirability of paying rent as a fixed percentage of revenue instead of a fixed amount – it's better to pay higher-than-market rent if actual business is better than forecast, than to be stuck with a fixed rental expense when actual business volume falls below projections. KFC also learned a lot about how to attract new customers, increase usage frequency of loyal customers, and reduce restaurants' operating expenses while not affecting the quality of food, service, and the customer experience. The biggest payoff from this rescue effort was not the restaurants turned around, or shut down, as the case might be. Rather, the biggest benefit came from the experience acquired, the lessons learned, which went far in minimizing, if not removing, similar mistakes from being repeated in the future. After all, the objective of KFC China is not simply accelerated growth, but profitable, accelerated growth.

Risks of Cannibalization and Market Saturation

In the process of analyzing the decline of average restaurant revenue and profit margin, the real estate committee identified cannibalization as one of the causes. The problem of cannibalization is caused by two or more KFC restaurants being located too close to each other and unintentionally competing against each other. It's a problem that, in a high-growth market like China, eventually disappears in most cases as a result of natural market growth. While there are experience-based rules of thumb that can be relied on to minimize short-term cannibalization, there is no fixed formula that can be depended on to avoid it entirely. In fact, today in Shanghai, five separate KFC restaurants can be found within a fraction of a mile from each other around a single square, all of which are generating high-volume business. There are other situations where the introduction of a second KFC restaurant in the same city, miles apart from the first, has produced a significant diluting impact on the revenue and profit margins of both.

Another risk closely related to cannibalization is market saturation, even in China's rapidly growing economy. At the macro-economic level, China as a fast-growing national economy has proven to be able to "digest" several hundred new KFC restaurants each year without any problem. However, at the micro-economic level – that is, at the level of individual cities and townships – the problem of market saturation can, and does, arise. Some cities and townships are more saturated than others due to differences in population, average income, purchasing power and propensity, and number and location of existing KFC and competing restaurants. In general, as the number of KFC and competing restaurants in a city rises to a point of critical mass, the risk of market saturation rises in proportion to the intensity of internal cannibalization and external competition. Since the big cities in eastern China such as Shanghai, Beijing, and Guangzhou represent the biggest market opportunities, they also attract the most restaurant brands from around the world, intensifying local competition and market saturation. In fact, as KFC China began to re-evaluate franchising in the late 1990s, this was one of the reasons for keeping franchisees out of the big cities – for their own protection.

As KFC China continues its rapid expansion, temporary decline in the average restaurant revenue and profit margin in select markets due to either cannibalization or market saturation is unavoidable.

When it happens, experiences gained by the real estate committee in the aftermath of the Asian financial crisis are still being used as a reference benchmark, a point of reflection for lessons learned and actions going forward.

FRANCHISING

The entire QSR industry is built on the concept of franchise. Of the major international fast-food restaurant brands such as Burger King, KFC, McDonald's, Pizza Hut, and Subway, every single one of them franchises more restaurants than it owns. Worldwide, in the case of KFC, the ratio between franchised versus company-owned restaurant units is roughly 10:1; in China, it's 1:20. An industry bias in favor of the franchise business model has been long standing, and for good business reasons. The name of the game is to leverage not only capital, but also management experience, entrepreneurial energy, local contacts and knowledge. From the moment Tricon was spun off from PepsiCo in 1997, there has been a persistent influence from the corporate headquarters in the U.S. for KFC China to pursue a more active program of franchising. The problem is, conditions for effective franchising did not exist in China back in the 1990s. The conditions are better today, but still not anywhere close to those found in the more developed world. The problem arises mostly due to the lack of qualified KFC franchisees, inadequate protection of trademarks and intellectual property rights (IPR), the lack of a legal infrastructure built around the protection of IPR with effective enforcement, and a cultural environment grossly lacking respect for IPR, making it hard to find qualified individual local franchisees who would comply strictly to the terms of a franchise agreement.

Within KFC China, some felt franchising was not the most effective model for profit maximization. One question often asked is, why give up 20 percent or more profit margin of a company-owned restaurant in exchange for a 6 percent royalty fee from a franchised restaurant? More importantly, why take on the risk of losing control over food and service quality and brand reputation, not to mention potential disagreement with a franchisee over operating values, company policies, and business practices? In the end, Dallas won out over Shanghai in this internal debate, and a program that marked the rebirth of franchising in KFC China finally began in 1999. It was a rebirth because the first and only KFC franchisee in China up to that point was established in Xian six years earlier, under very different circumstances, as previously discussed in Chapter 4.

KFC China's born-again franchise program was kicked off internally in early 1999. Due to its strategic importance and experimental nature, the program remained a project within the YUM! Greater China Executive Committee during the first year. In the first round of internal discussions, the Executive Committee quickly tackled the question of defining the criteria for franchisee screening and selection, based on our knowledge of the local market condition. The committee never bothered with setting any short-term or long-term quantifiable goals because it was felt that, given the uncertainty surrounding the topic of franchising in China, the project was an experiment – a feasibility study. The screening criteria for a prospective franchisee, which the committee identified early on, included:

1. an entrepreneur with restaurant, preferably QSR, industry experience;
2. who was willing to play a hands-on role in the management of a KFC restaurant, not just be a financial investor. Therefore, if he or she was not already a resident of a city in which a KFC restaurant to be franchised was located, he or she would be willing and prepared to relocate to that city; and
3. who would invest a significant sum out of his or her personal net worth. If necessary, he or she could borrow from either a bank or from YUM! Brands.

The committee spent time on the discussion of what type of KFC restaurant should be franchised, and how KFC would support a franchisee from initial training and system orientation to on-going operational support covering all functional activities. Should KFC franchise new or existing restaurants, or both? In which KFC market(s) and cities? Would KFC provide a franchisee with a path for growth, and if so, how? In the end, the Executive Committee decided KFC would only re-franchise existing restaurants that were being operated profitably in medium-size cities with a growth potential for additional KFC restaurants in the foreseeable future. The committee also decided that KFC would begin this experiment geographically close to Shanghai so that support could be provided by the Shanghai Restaurant Support Center directly rather than through any of the KFC markets. Each operating KFC restaurant would be re-franchised at the cost of approximately US$1 million to a prospective franchisee, plus a small one-time franchise fee, an ongoing royalty fee of 6 percent of revenue, and a marketing fee of 4 percent. In return, a franchisee would receive a profitable, operating restaurant and all assets associated with the ongoing operation of that restaurant, including the entire restaurant staff if so desired. This saved a franchisee from having to select a restaurant site, negotiate a lease agreement, oversee restaurant construction, recruit and train employees, and source supplies, thus reducing operational as well as financial risks, with a much stronger prospect for financial success compared to building a new restaurant from scratch in a big city.

At the beginning KFC did not want to open a floodgate of enquiries while still in the experimental stage. So, the news was selectively released that KFC China was reviewing potential franchisees through a few carefully selected channels. Within a month or two the Executive Committee was interviewing prospective candidates. The committee stuck close to its screening criteria, believing that the success of the first few cases would be critical to the program's future viability. Not surprisingly, almost all candidates were ethnic Chinese from overseas. Eventually, the committee picked a man who had spent years in Taiwan and the U.S. with lots of fast-food restaurant experience to be the first KFC franchisee in China under the new franchise business model.

For many months before KFC China turned over an existing KFC restaurant located in Li-Yang, Jiangsu Province, to this new franchisee in August 2000, I led one of my last cross-functional projects at KFC to develop a complete franchisee support system and associated documentation targeting all future KFC franchisees in China. Within weeks after the new franchisee support system commenced operation I left KFC. Later, I heard the same franchisee acquired franchise rights to additional KFC restaurants, an indication of a satisfactory financial return, and a good enough fit with KFC's system, values, and practices. Today, the KFC franchise program in China remains small in scope, with only a few dozen franchised restaurant units out of a total of over 2,000 at the beginning of 2008. However, the situation may change as KFC China gears up its franchise program by lowering the financial entry hurdle of US$1 million by as much as 75 percent, which was announced to the public in April 2006. Looking ahead, this announcement may yet bring profound implications for KFC, its competitors, franchisees, and customers in the decades ahead.

CONCLUSION

During its first 20 years, KFC China opened 2,000 restaurants, generating on average 20 percent gross profit margin per restaurant, and achieved its strategy of profitable growth at maximum speed. Clearly, successful execution of this strategy required committed, dedicated teamwork from all internal functions and employees as well as external partners. Of them, one internal function, real estate development, stands out as the most visible, if not the most significant, contributor to the outstanding execution of this strategy.

The evolution of the real estate development function of KFC China reflects, once again, the flexibility, innovativeness, and adaptability inherent in KFC China's "DNA," continuously modifying and improving the current business model based on newly acquired data and experience. Thus far, this predominantly direct investment model for restaurant expansion has been sufficient to support KFC China's growth target. Looking ahead, will this direct-investment business model be able to support future growth aspirations? If not, what are the required remedial actions and associated risks? These are questions that will be addressed in Chapter 12.

8

OPERATIONAL EXCELLENCE

INTRODUCTION

Within weeks of joining KFC, as part of my new employee orientation program, I spent a full week in a KFC restaurant and a distribution center in the city of Nanjing, a market fully owned by YUM! Brands with a reputation for operational excellence. In the restaurant I was rotated through different work stations in the kitchen, preparing the Hot-and-Spicy Chicken Wings, the Hot-and-Spicy Sandwich, otherwise known internally as "The Zinger" – two of KFC China's best-selling products – plus the Original Recipe, the French fries, and the cobbed corn. Later, I was rotated through behind-the-counter workstations to man the cash register, ice cream and soda dispensers, and other assignments in the back room to inspect in-restaurant storage of dry, cooled, and frozen food and incoming supplies delivered by the KFC Nanjing distribution center.

This practice of rotating a newcomer through a KFC restaurant's operation reflects an industry practice, as well as KFC's company culture: a front-line-centered culture. Embedded in this culture is an intense focus on customers – both internal and external – and their needs and satisfaction. From my first day at KFC, I knew that a very important part of my job was to rally my colleagues in the Shanghai Restaurant Support Center around a mission to provide the best support possible to all KFC restaurants in China.

FRONT-LINE CENTERED AND CUSTOMER FOCUSED

Shortly after joining KFC, I noticed a phenomenon deeply rooted in Chinese culture. Some of my colleagues working in the Shanghai headquarters perceived themselves as a cut above those working outside Shanghai, and acted accordingly in daily interactions. There were several causes for this attitude. First, the headquarters mentality reminiscent of China's almighty imperial court dating back to the dynastic era no doubt played a role. Second, an attitude held by some Shanghai residents toward "country folks" from other parts of China. Third, KFC's internal salary grade structure and higher income reflecting Shanghai's higher cost of living also contributed to a misperception of differentiation, if not superiority.

Instead of viewing KFC's Shanghai office as primarily a service provider for all KFC markets in China, some employees based in Shanghai viewed it more as headquarters where command and control originated. Worse yet, some of our employees in the field agreed with this view, a natural product of a few thousand years of feudalism. Changes were needed, fast.

First, KFC's Shanghai office became, officially, Shanghai Restaurant Support Center in order to better reflect its true mission and YUM! Brands' corporate values. Next, members of the Executive Committee set about explaining the role of Shanghai Restaurant Support Center to employees, especially those based in Shanghai, emphasizing the "service provider" aspect of our role. Then, senior management made a point of going out of their way to respond to field requests expeditiously, giving them the highest priority. On important and urgent field issues, it was essential to pull the team in Shanghai Restaurant Support Center together and work around the clock for hours or sometimes even days until a solution was delivered and implemented. Soon, colleagues in and outside Shanghai got the point. Shanghai Restaurant Support Center became what it is now, a service and support provider, in name and in deeds.

Exhibit 12: A KFC Restaurant in Shanghai

Restaurant Economics

Exhibit 12 illustrates an average KFC restaurant in Shanghai. Of all KFC restaurants around the world, China has some of the busiest, and the most profitable. The average KFC restaurant in China generates over a thousand sales transactions per day and produces over US$1 million of revenue per year at a restaurant profit margin of 20 percent or more. This is despite the fact that a portion of the cost of labor is attributable to "double decking" the restaurant management team necessary for on-the-job training in preparation for opening new restaurants. Compared to KFC China, the average KFC restaurant in the U.S. generates less than half as many transactions per day and produces US$900,000 of annual revenue at a profit margin of less than 15 percent.

Exhibit 13 lists the cost of goods sold (food, paper, etc.), cost of labor (payroll, employee benefits, etc.), and cost of occupancy and other operating expenses (rent, utilities, etc.) among YUM! Brands' U.S., China, and international divisions between the years 2003 to 2006. It provides an interesting comparison among three very different markets over a four-year period. The dynamic nature of the China market in comparison to the U.S. and the rest of the world can be glimpsed through the figures in Exhibit 13.

The average profit margin of KFC restaurants in China is significantly higher than that of KFC restaurants elsewhere around the world. While the cost of purchased food and materials and the cost of restaurant leasing are proportionally higher, the cost of labor in China is significantly lower. This should be a surprise to no one. The abundance of low-cost labor has been a major contributor to China's emergence as the "world's factory" in the past three decades. A word of caution is warranted here: low-cost labor does not equate to low-quality labor. In fact, within KFC's worldwide restaurant operation, China has been consistently singled out as a leader in setting and delivering high restaurant operation standards in recent years.

CHAMPS

To maintain a consistently high standard on operational speed, food and service quality, and restaurant cleanliness day in and day out in a fast-moving market environment requires an experienced, well-

Exhibit 13: KFC Restaurant Economics

2003	USA	China	International	Worldwide
Sales	100%	100%	100%	100%
Food & Paper	28.80%	38.00%	34.10%	30.90%
Payroll & Employee Benefits	31.00%	10.70%	23.80%	27.20%
Occupancy & Other Operating Expenses	25.60%	31.50%	29.10%	27.10%
Restaurant Margin	14.60%	19.80%	13.00%	14.80%

2004	USA	China	International	Worldwide
Sales	100%	100%	100%	100%
Food & Paper	29.90%	37.10%	33.80%	31.80%
Payroll & Employee Benefits	30.50%	11.50%	23.80%	26.40%
Occupancy & Other Operating Expenses	25.80%	31.10%	29.40%	27.30%
Restaurant Margin	13.80%	20.30%	13.00%	14.50%

2005	USA	China	International	Worldwide
Sales	100%	100%	100%	100%
Food & Paper	29.80%	36.20%	33.10%	31.40%
Payroll & Employee Benefits	30.20%	13.30%	24.10%	26.40%
Occupancy & Other Operating Expenses	26.20%	33.10%	30.70%	28.20%
Restaurant Margin	13.80%	17.40%	12.10%	14.00%

2006	USA	China	International	Worldwide
Sales	100%	100%	100%	100%
Food & Paper	28.20%	35.40%	32.20%	30.50%
Payroll & Employee Benefits	30.10%	12.90%	24.60%	25.60%
Occupancy & Other Operating Expenses	27.10%	31.30%	31.00%	28.70%
Restaurant Margin	14.60%	20.40%	12.20%	15.20%

Source: YUM! Brands 2005 & 2006 Annual Report

trained, and motivated workforce, guided by a thorough, well-tested system for restaurant operation management. In KFC, this system is called CHAMPS, short for Cleanliness, Hospitality, Accuracy, Maintenance, Product quality, and Speed.

Cleanliness. Various consumer surveys have reported that one of the most important reasons for many Chinese consumers frequenting KFC restaurants is the interior environment, from a restaurant's colors, lighting, music, decorations, temperature, air flow, and scent to the cleanliness of its windows, trays, countertops, floors, tables, and chairs, all the way to the hand-washing basin and the toilet. Yes, the toilet. Over the years, many foreign visitors to China have learned, the hard way, to avoid having to use local toilets unless, of course, it's a toilet inside a KFC or McDonald's. Local Chinese consumers know that they can rely on consistently clean and sanitary condition of a toilet in any KFC restaurant, anywhere, any time. How does KFC manage this? After all, the "hardware" in a KFC toilet is not plush or outstanding, its size often small and cramped. It's the result of hard work by a well-trained, well-disciplined, and well-managed restaurant crew to keep every corner of a restaurant clean throughout the day, especially during busy hours. It's also the result of a detailed, well-defined, and well-executed operational system and process, including a timetable and a set of prescribed procedures in detail for toilet cleaning. Details of each restaurant's daily operation is written into the restaurant operation manual, down to which lights to put on first thing in the morning, how many minutes prior to restaurant opening, and in what sequence. As a result, stepping into a KFC restaurant in China means to an average Chinese consumer that he or she can expect a clean, relaxed, well-lit dining environment with pleasant music and polite service, anywhere, any time.

Hospitality. Today, in many restaurants throughout China you will be greeted at the door as you enter, "Welcome to XYZ!" Prior to the mid-1990s, it was unheard of. Many of these restaurants learned from KFC. For years, KFC restaurant employees have been trained to greet every customer who walks into a KFC restaurant with "Welcome to KFC!" At first, it was simply a slogan. Later, after repeated discussions in the KFC Shanghai Restaurant Support Center on how to make such greetings perceived by customers as sincerely coming from the heart of a KFC employee rather than sounding like an automatic recording, a decision was made to incorporate into all future restaurant crew training instructions on how best to greet customers. It's never easy to perfect employee attitude and behavior toward customers, but oftentimes a company culture of respect for employees needs to be developed first.

Sometimes, a KFC restaurant's hospitality extends beyond a restaurant into its surrounding community – through donations and program sponsorship in schools and hospitals, for example, generating community goodwill and improving public relations.

Accuracy. All KFC restaurant team members behind the counter are taught to repeat an order after it has been placed by a customer in order to ensure order accuracy. They are also trained to remind a customer to trade up by suggesting a new product, a combination meal, a soft drink, a snack, a dessert, and so on. Before receiving a customer's payment, a crew member will read out loud the total ordered amount. After receiving payment, a crew member will read out loud the amount paid, and the amount of change in return. All of this is part of KFC's employee training to ensure order accuracy.

Maintenance. Regular equipment maintenance is the responsibility of each KFC restaurant, with equipment manufacturers and their representatives responsible for repairs and periodic safety checkups. Throughout the 1980s and 1990s, the kitchens in all KFC restaurants in China were dominated by several friers for the preparation of fried chicken and French fries. In the early 2000s, an oven was added to enable each restaurant to prepare new non-fried products such as Portuguese egg tarts and roasted chicken, greatly expanding the variety of potential new product offerings. In addition to kitchen equipment, all furniture, children's toys, windows, doors, lighting, air-conditioning, bathroom facilities, exterior signage, etc. need regular maintenance. A local repair team, usually outsourced, is on-call daily to ensure preventive measures are taken periodically and, when needed, repairs are completed immediately in order to avoid any disruption in a restaurant's normal business operation.

Product quality. Of all the important features reported by Chinese customers that attract them to a particular restaurant, quality of food ranks at the top. In the case of KFC, quality of food begins with effective application of the STAR system based on which all suppliers are periodically evaluated on multiple dimensions such as food quality, safety, reliability, consistency, technology, conformity to standards in production, storage, and shipment. In addition to the supply chain, another key contributor to perceived product quality lies in food preparation inside each KFC restaurant. For a given product, all restaurant crew members are trained to use the same equipment, based on the same operation procedure, down to the exact second of cooking time. Every batch of cooked but unsold products is kept in warm storage, up to a time limit beyond which it is discarded. This procedure is expected to be enforced strictly in every KFC restaurant in order to maintain high, and consistent, food quality throughout China.

Many Chinese consumers prefer tongue-burning fried chicken fresh out of the frier. Try a piece of KFC fried chicken fresh out of the frier next time you are in China. Many of my friends and relatives visiting China for the first time tell me they taste better than KFC fried chicken found anywhere else around the world.

Speed. Throughout KFC China's relatively short history, different KFC world records for individual restaurants such as maximum seating capacity, daily traffic volume, and number of meals served per day have been broken. At one time, KFC's first restaurant in China located at Qianmen near Tiananmen Square in Beijing occupied three floors with 800 seats. Speed of service at peak hours in a "fast" food restaurant of this size becomes a really interesting test case. Crowds can pack in front of a counter layers deep, which sometimes seems even more crowded than a major sports event.

Effectively handling peak-hour traffic when customers wait in line layers deep, which in some KFC restaurants can happen several times a day, requires careful interior restaurant design, high speed of service, and special procedures to shorten waiting time in long queues. KFC China trains all restaurant crew members to complete a single counter transaction, from the moment of first greeting to the moment a customer walks away from the counter with food ordered, in 60 seconds. On top of that, it's expected to be done with a smile on the face and a welcoming attitude from the heart, consistent throughout the day, day in and day out.

Within KFC China, each restaurant is measured on financial objectives such as revenue, profit margin, and growth. In addition, there are various measurements of restaurant operational excellence. For example, each KFC restaurant in China is inspected, evaluated, and graded once a month based on a long list of measurement criteria derived from CHAMPS. In fact, the overall grade tallied up at the end of each such inspection is called a CHAMPS score, which in turn becomes an important base for the annual performance evaluation of a KFC restaurant and its management staff. Another measurement device of restaurant operational excellence is the mystery shopper.

Mystery Shopper

Based on an extension of the premise that "a job that is measured gets done well," the concept of mystery shopper assumes that "a job that is measured impromptu gets done well all of the time." Well, perhaps not all of the time, but there is little doubt that the mystery shopper program does catch the attention of KFC's restaurant operation staff. The fact that the mystery shopper program score is an integral part of a KFC restaurant management team's annual performance evaluation process further enhances its perceived importance. So, what is a mystery shopper program?

Simply put, a mystery shopper program is a quality assurance program that KFC uses as a tool to measure, and to ensure, customer satisfaction. The program is managed by KFC China's QA department, but outsourced to a third-party company. The third-party recruits and trains "mystery shoppers" to visit, unannounced, all KFC restaurants year-round. Each mystery shopper goes through the entire sales cycle the same as the average KFC customer does, with one big difference – the mystery shopper has an extra mission. Unlike the average customer, a mystery shopper secretly scores a KFC restaurant's performance based on a long list of measurement criteria that includes elements of cleanliness, food quality, service attitude, service time, and speed – in other words, key elements of CHAMPS, the core of KFC China's restaurant operation management system. Because a mystery shopper can show up any time unannounced in a KFC restaurant, it keeps a well-motivated restaurant staff focused on key elements of CHAMPS all of the time, which, in turn, leads to customer satisfaction.

Customer Mania

YUM! Brands rolled out a restaurant operation program called Customer Mania during 2002 in order to further improve customer satisfaction and encourage repeat business by empowering employees to make on-the-spot decisions on behalf of customers. In their own words, YUM! Brands is committed to driving an operating culture where everything they do is centered on their customers – focused on customer satisfaction, every customer, every time.

One customer segment that has received extra attention from KFC China from the very beginning is children. This means, of course, broad organizational impact affecting multiple functions such as purchasing and marketing, but no function is more affected than restaurant operation. This is because all children-targeted programs and activities, with the exception of advertising, take place inside KFC restaurants. They include children's birthday parties; children's drawing contests, writing composition contests, and other contests; sales promotions such as kids' meals and free or discounted toys; singing and dancing led by restaurant hostesses; and Chicky – the KFC mascot. The kids' program is so important to KFC China, in fact, that dedicated staff with special training have become a part of the normal restaurant operation management system.

MARKET GENERAL MANAGER

In addition to well-tested restaurant management systems such as CHAMPS and mystery shopper, another key factor for KFC restaurants' operational success lies in the qualifications of KFC China's first-generation market general managers, almost all of whom were members of the "Taiwan Gang." During KFC China's first decade, a group of influential and powerful market general managers – "field commanders" – emerged. They are driven, entrepreneurial, and well-experienced fast-food industry veterans who have learned their trade in another ethnic Chinese market environment earlier in their career. They were challenged to build a KFC market from the ground up, and to build as big and as fast as they could within their respective territory. They did.

Under these circumstances, it is no wonder that the organizational change initiated in 1997 to centralize all restaurant support functions, and to establish systems and processes in preparation for the next phase of growth, met with strong resistance from many market general managers. In the end, their initial resistance was ameliorated through a number of measures, most notably by keeping all market general managers' profit and loss responsibility intact. That is, while field logistics and distribution, purchasing, and other restaurant support functions no longer reported to them, they still retained a personal incentive to actively monitor the performance of these functions in order to ensure products and service of maximum quality are delivered to all restaurants timely, efficiently, and at minimum cost. Their input, especially on issues of rising cost or declining quality of products and service delivered by these restaurant support functions, are actively solicited at all times, including at each year's annual performance evaluation time. In other words, with regard to these restaurant support functions, the role of a market general manager has gone from being a boss to being a customer – an internal customer. While a customer is always right, you can't say the same about a boss. In the end, the smartest market general managers began to realize that sometimes it's better to be an internal customer than to be a boss.

Removing the direct management responsibility for these restaurant support functions from market general managers allowed them to spend more time and effort to focus on the two most critically important business objectives for themselves, for the KFC markets they lead, and for YUM! Brands. They are: to maximize customer satisfaction in each and every KFC restaurant, every day; and to maximize rapid and profitable restaurant growth.

Since the beginning of this century, as members of the first-generation market general managers retired, resigned, or were re-assigned, more and more locally trained market general managers have risen through the ranks. This is perhaps the greatest of all achievements made by the first-generation market general managers as they led, coached, and prepped their local successors over the years until the latter were ready for the baton. Frankly, I do not envy the position of the second, and future, generations of market general managers. Their predecessors have created an impressive track record that's tough to beat.

RGM IS NUMBER ONE

By early 2008, only three of KFC China's first-generation market general managers remained in the field, out of a total of over a dozen. All of the second-generation market general managers have risen through KFC restaurant operation's organizational hierarchy, beginning with management trainee, advancing through assistant restaurant manager, deputy restaurant manager, restaurant general manager, area manager, district manager, and, finally, market general manager. This, by itself, is a strong testimony to the success of KFC China's employee training and development program.

Within this restaurant operation organizational hierarchy, one position is especially critical, some say even more so than the market general manager, and that is the role of a restaurant general manager, or RGM for short. The reason is simple. On an average day, a few million customers walk into KFC restaurants throughout China. A KFC restaurant is not only where these customer interfaces – these "moments of truth" – take place every single day, it's also a factory where the physical product – the food and drinks – are "manufactured," as well as a retail outlet where food and service are dispensed and consumed. In other words, a restaurant is where all of the interactions with customers take place, where "the rubber meets the road."

To safeguard millions of customer satisfactions each day, 365 days a year (some KFC restaurants in China are closed early for the Chinese New Year's Eve) requires a well-trained, well-disciplined, and well-motivated workforce. The average KFC restaurant in China provides job opportunities for many dozens to a few hundred employees. They all report to an RGM.

All RGMs play a unique and important role of being direct links between restaurant employees and customers. It's a critical link. On one hand, through the link to customers, an effective RGM can ensure customer satisfaction, repeat business, and financial success for a restaurant. On the other hand, through the link to employees, an effective RGM can ensure employee satisfaction, high quality service, high employee productivity, and restaurant financial performance.

A KFC RGM in China carries a huge responsibility. Often, a KFC China RGM is in his or her twenties. Not too many business enterprises in China or, for that matter, anywhere around the world, can offer a young person at that tender age career opportunities of comparable impact on (hundreds, even thousands of) customers, (dozens of) employees, and (million-dollar-per-year) financial statements every day.

Because of the importance of this position to the company's success, RGMs in YUM! Brands belong to an exclusive club. At least once a year, they are the focus of attention during a multiple-day event designed for training, motivation, recognition, and celebration called the RGM Conference. It can be an emotional event filled with slogan chanting, flag waving, and tear shedding, comparable to the famed emotion-filled Wal-Mart employee gatherings led by Sam Walton. In recognition of the importance of RGMs' contributions to the company's future, YUM! Brands coined the term "RGM #1" years ago and began granting RGMs company stock options.

Each year, RGMs with CHAMPS scores ranked in the top tier, and their partners from all over the world are invited to participate in a celebration called the Champion's Club. The best of the RGMs dream of being invited to this event, the highest honor and recognition attainable among their peers from all over the world.

CONCLUSION

It has not been easy for KFC China to grow from one to 2,000 restaurants in 20 years, nor has it been easy to successfully manage so many restaurants, day in and day out, in such a vast and diverse country without too many major hiccups. On the first accomplishment – rapid restaurant expansion – much credit should go to the first-generation KFC market general managers. These pioneers rich in industry experience and knowledge of China laid down the structural backbone for later market expansion during KFC China's first decade. On the second accomplishment, much credit should go to CHAMPS, mystery shopper, and other restaurant operation management systems and programs.

While size, speed and growth have been KFC China's best friends in the past, they may also become KFC China's biggest enemies in the future. Each KFC restaurant resembles a small company with its own management team, labor force, and support infrastructure. As the number of restaurants continues to grow, it becomes more and more difficult to maintain a high level of consistency of operational values and practices across the board. Incidents reported during 2005 suggesting a pattern in some KFC restaurants of deliberate violation of quality standards by selling products beyond expiration should have sounded a major alarm.

Going forward, how to maintain the high-speed growth momentum without sacrificing quality performance, especially inside thousands of KFC restaurants where millions of "moment of truth" take place each day, will be a major challenge facing KFC China for years to come.

9

LOCALIZATION AND GLOBALIZATION

THE THREE PHASES OF KFC CHINA

From the perspective of the evolution of an organization, KFC China went through at least three different phases in the first 20 years of its history. Phase One lasted from 1987 to 1997 during which major market hubs were established at strategic locations throughout China under a highly decentralized and fragmented organizational structure. Phase Two, a period of centralization and systemization, began in 1997 and continued into the early 2000s, with emphasis placed on the establishment and solidification of management systems, processes, and standards in order to manage the workforce, materials, and information flows more efficiently. Phase Three, which began in 2002, has been marked by a rapid expansion at the pace of several hundred new restaurants per year, combined with an equally rapid stream of new and localized product introductions.

Phase One – Building Market Hubs

During Phase One, KFC China's focus was on the creation of a geographic market framework in order to lay down the infrastructure to enable future, large-scale restaurant expansion. By 1997, 18 KFC markets had been established throughout China. The geographic market framework was largely in place, waiting to be loaded with a critical mass of new restaurants in order to reap the economic and marketing benefits of scale and efficiency. To encourage maximum speed, each KFC market was given full autonomy, profit and loss accountability, self-sufficient resources, and few cross-market bonding and sharing mechanisms during the first ten years. By 1997, these autonomous markets had by and large accomplished the primary mission of their time, laying down the structural foundation for future restaurant expansion across China. Ironically, having successfully facilitated the evolution of Phase One, this organizational structure was ill-fitted for the next phase, which required a transformation of KFC China from an invincible guerrilla force into a well-trained, well-disciplined, and well-organized professional army.

Phase Two – Building Management Systems, Processes, and Organizational Capabilities

The primary focus of Phase Two was to consolidate the gains and the lessons learned from Phase One and to develop organizational structure, management systems, processes, and talents into an efficient combination capable of opening hundreds, instead of dozens, of new restaurants every year. A new, centralized organizational structure was put in place to strengthen all restaurant support functions critical to a successful push for restaurant expansion – warehousing, transportation, purchasing, supplier management, information technology, quality assurance, and real estate development. In each of these functions, systems and processes adapted to China based on years of local experience were vigorously implemented. New systems were developed when required.

In addition to the introduction and implementation of various management systems and processes, another element of KFC's focus during Phase Two was employee training and organizational capability development. For example, during 1998, seven high-potential employees in various functions were transferred, mostly between the Shanghai Restaurant Support Center and different KFC markets, as part of their personal career development program. KFC's interest in employee training and organizational capability development went further beyond high-potential employees. As described in Chapter 2, KFC's projects included the introduction of an on-site company library in every KFC market office, hosting lunch-time brown-bag sessions open to all employees, and introducing courses on general business topics – in addition to restaurant operations – such as project management and time management, from which all employees could benefit.

I was so deeply committed to employee career development that I even pushed the one employee whose assistance I needed the most on to her preferred career track. This was done with a lot of pain, but little regret. Those who have had the privilege of serving in an executive capacity in big companies would probably agree that, of all employees on your staff, losing your personal assistant would cause the greatest pain. In early 2000, I facilitated a career transfer for Jessica, my able personal assistant who had worked with me for over two years. Earlier, during my first interview with Jessica, she'd told me that her career interest did not stop at being an executive assistant. Rather, her long-term career interest lay in human resource management. I promised Jessica that I would assist her in the realization of her career goals once she had proven herself worthy. In the ensuing two years, I kept in mind Jessica's career interest, getting her involved in HR-related task forces, asking her to work with me on HR-related projects as much as I could. Meanwhile, Jessica took professional, HR-related courses inside and outside YUM! Brands, some on her own time. All the while, Jessica delivered a superb job performance. In the end, with great pain, I was extremely happy to wish Jessica off on her next career stop, in the human resource department of the Shanghai Restaurant Support Center.

Phase Three – Expansion at Full Speed

Phase Three is marked by a remarkable growth of new KFC restaurants at the rate of a few hundred every year beginning in 2002, with more than 2,000 in place by year-end 2007, and still growing fast. Phase Three is also marked by a continuation of the localization strategy across the board, with emphasis on brand positioning and new product introduction. In the past few years, Phase Three has shown new signs of pressure stemming from the rising expectations for growth from YUM! Brands worldwide headquarters, signs including the increasingly arduous search for a fourth growth engine beyond KFC, Pizza Hut, and Pizza Hut Express.

In Phase Three, the top-down approach no longer works as well as in the earlier phases due simply to size. Decentralization, delegation of power and authority, breaking up a growing headquarters bureaucracy, and keeping business units small and agile will become inevitable as growth continues.

PUTTING SYSTEMS AND PROCESSES IN PLACE

During its first ten years – Phase One – KFC China was the equivalent of a loosely bounded federation of local fiefdoms high on entrepreneurial drive but low on systemization, standardization, discipline, and focus on quality, consistency, efficiency, and teamwork. During my first year with KFC, I focused on consolidating the restaurant support functions and putting various management systems and processes into practice, thus initiating Phase Two. Systems and processes such as the STAR system, new product development process, real estate development review and approval process, franchisee support system, crisis management system, MBO system, employee training and development system, management succession system, and mentoring system were introduced or reintroduced, and practiced with vigor, solidifying their place within the organization on a permanent basis.

The collective leadership team of KFC China in 1997 was a group of highly skilled and motivated entrepreneurs with rich battlefield experience, not unlike a collection of strong, independent, and battle-scarred guerrilla force commanders. What KFC needed in order to fight and win the much bigger battles that lay ahead included a unified direction; a systems approach to business management; strong discipline to execute according to systems and standards with built-in flexibility to reflect shifting market dynamics; and cross-unit coordination and communication in order to leverage their collective size and combined strengths. A bigger challenge was to fill in these missing links and to do so without slowing down the speed of growth, dampening the entrepreneurial spirit, or suppressing other positive organizational "genes" such as speed, decisiveness, flexibility, innovativeness, risk-taking, and bias for action.

Managing Efficiency

To put localized management systems and procedures in place and to enforce them earnestly does not require a growing organizational bureaucracy; nor does rapidly expanding business volume. During my years with KFC, I kept the growth of KFC's staff headcount extremely tight, especially at the Shanghai Restaurant Support Center. With the exception of real estate development, none of the other functions under my direct responsibility experienced any noticeable headcount increase during those years. I wanted to keep Shanghai headquarters staff at a minimum so that they didn't get in the way of productive employees in the field.

In addition to keeping an eye on headcount, I also kept a close watch on big investment projects. Major investment proposals such as the design and construction of new KFC restaurants, purchase of new delivery trucks, consolidation and expansion of existing warehouses, construction of new warehouses, and facility upgrades received careful scrutiny on both cost-effectiveness and timing of investment from me before they were passed on to finance for approval. I did so not only because it was part of making the right business decisions, but also with the hope that my colleagues would take my actions to heart so that in the future these systems, processes, methods, and decision criteria would be kept alive and improved upon, continuously.

LOCALIZATION AND GLOBALIZATION

The business model for a QSR chain is a "cookie cutter" business model. That is, in order to present a consistent consumer experience and brand image around the world, all restaurants, although situated in different countries and cities, facing different social, cultural, political and economic contexts, adopt a common "look and feel" through common standards and practices. Yet, beyond this common appearance, some local adaptations and adjustments are necessary, appropriate, and unavoidable. McDonald's introduction of vegetable burgers in India and other vegetarian markets is an excellent, oft-cited, example.

Common standards and practices exist in McDonald's, KFC, Wendy's, Subway, and all other successful QSR chains out of necessity. Without common standards on restaurant design, layout, fixtures, colors, signage and logo display, different KFC restaurants would run the risk of projecting different brand images to the same customer. Without common standards on employee uniforms, behaviors, and restaurant operating procedures, different KFC restaurants would produce different customer experiences. Without common standards for equipment, facility, and operating procedure for the storage, cooking, and dispensing of finished products, different KFC restaurants would deliver finished products in different appearances, tastes, and customer perceptions. In fact, lack of standards implies lack of consistency, anathema in an industry built on consistency, efficiency, speed, and quality.

Where should a multinational corporation draw the line between global standardization in order to derive global economic efficiency and brand consistency on one hand, and local adaptation in order to better meet local market needs on the other? In China, as elsewhere, the optimal choice is seldom one or the other. Instead, it is a question of degree and mix. And it is situation-dependent.

Both KFC and McDonald's operate far-flung fast-food restaurant operations around the world with success. Both have developed "cookie cutting" systems, policies, and procedures that have been proven to work.

Nevertheless, there are significant differences, in value as well as in practice, between KFC and McDonald's application of these "cookie cutting" systems, policies, and procedures – at least in China. These differences range from the location of their China headquarters to policies on products and partnerships. Until 2005, McDonald's China headquarters were in Hong Kong, while KFC relocated its China headquarters from Hong Kong to Shanghai in the 1990s. Early on, McDonald's invited U.S.-based product and service suppliers providing everything from hamburger buns to distribution and logistics service to go to China to build a McDonald's supply chain, while KFC opted to rely much more on developing local supply partners. These examples provide just a few telltale signs of differing practices and underlying values, with clues for their preference regarding the degree of globalization versus localization for their respective operations in China.

The McDonald's Way

If the first ten years of KFC's operation in China can be described as that of a guerrilla force, then McDonald's can only be described as that of a regular army. We've already cited McDonald's decision early on to bring its strategic partners for critical products and services to China ahead of its first restaurant opening in China. This decision was no doubt driven by the fact that no local supplier could be found at the time to provide these products and services in China that met McDonald's high quality standards. I couldn't help but wonder, though, whether this decision also has been the result of a line of thinking that goes: this is the way we do things around the world – and it has worked – why should we do things differently in China?

In any event, since their arrival in China, McDonald's and its strategic partners have made huge capital investments, reflecting not only their intention to stay in China for the long haul, but also expectations for rapid growth. Unfortunately, their heavy, untimely investments combined with other factors led to a higher cost structure compared to KFC, thus contributing to a slowdown in the company's growth later, which in turn further exacerbated its uncompetitive cost structure due to inadequate scale. Is McDonald's China an example of an otherwise successful global monolith applying a tried and proven approach to a new market entry, but this time in a very different market?

The KFC Way

In contrast, KFC entered China with relatively few financial resources, but lots of flexibility, entrepreneurial drive, and innovative spirit.

During its first ten years in China, KFC operated relatively free of any formal system or success formula, relying instead on the best judgment of an industry-experienced and China-knowledgeable senior leadership team. It reminds me of a now-famous statement describing the process of China's economic reforms – "crossing the river by feeling the pebbles at the bottom." Later, only after a critical mass of business volume and operating experience had been accumulated inside China, was a serious attempt then made to put in place localized systems of various sorts to match the Chinese context.

The lessons we can draw from this brief comparison between McDonald's approach to China and KFC's approach to China include:

1. It's dangerous to assume that a given business model will work equally well around the world, especially in a market like China, which is so huge, complex, and different from the West, and changing so rapidly.
2. Sometimes the lack of a formal management system in the early stage of a new market entry is preferable to the early placement of management systems that have been proven elsewhere if market characteristics are unfamiliar, and changes dynamic.

Localization of Employees

China is a market with a long history and deeply entrenched culture. Any foreign company selling a product or service that touches upon the country's cultural "core"– such as food products or education services – must consider measures of localization unless it is content to stay within a niche market segment. On the other hand, selling a high-technology product such as a laptop PC in China requires relatively little localization effort beyond language translation, channels of distribution, and customer support because it's far less culture-sensitive. While the need for localization depends on the characteristics of market, a product or a service, the extent of localization depends on a company's willingness to localize, reflecting elements of its "DNA" such as flexibility and adaptability.

KFC's decision to adopt a broad and active localization strategy in China began with the assembly of the "Taiwan Gang," which was, practically speaking, as "local" a leadership team as feasible at the time. Once a qualified and experienced leadership team is in place that understands both the best industry practices outside China and the local context inside China, it is then in a position to make the best judgment, including how far, how deep, and how fast to go, on localization practices across people, products, functions, geographic units, systems, policies, and procedures. Their best judgment translates into timely action programs, many of which deviate from the parent corporation's worldwide policies and practices, which, in turn, requires corporate approval and support.

At the end of 2007, approximately 200,000 employees working in 2,000 KFC restaurants – including all 2,000 RGMs – throughout China were local Chinese, making KFC one of the largest private employers, if not THE largest, in China. By the end of this decade, as many more members of the "Taiwan Gang" approach retirement age and as local Chinese employees gradually replace them, the speed of localization at the top of KFC China's organizational structure will accelerate, and eventually the baton will be passed on to a truly local leadership team. It's only a matter of time.

This trend very much reflects the larger business environment in which KFC China competes, with very few exceptions. One recent exception is McDonald's. At the end of 2005 and the beginning of 2006, McDonald's replaced the top leadership team of its China operation, which caused tremors inside and out, as can be expected. What came next, however, surprised many industry observers. McDonald's decided to send two 30-year McDonald's veterans with little China knowledge or experience from McDonald's worldwide headquarters in Oak Brook, Illinois to oversee its China operation. It will be interesting to watch what McDonald's does next in China.

One reliable source estimates that, while none of the top positions of foreign companies in China were filled by local Chinese in the mid-1990s, by 2006, 70 percent of them were. The reasons are straightforward. Local hires cost less, as much as 80 percent less than expatriates, and have a better understanding of the local context. In recent years, a few local Chinese executives have even advanced to positions in Asia-Pacific or worldwide corporate headquarters of some multinational corporations.

Localization of Products and Supply Chain

Since KFC China's test kitchen was set up in Shanghai during the late 1990s, KFC has been busy with frequent new product introductions. Almost all of these new products have been designed with local Chinese characteristics in mind, from content and taste to appearance and name. Product names like Beijing Chicken Roll, Golden Butterfly Shrimp, Four Seasons Fresh Vegetable Salad, Fragrant Mushroom Rice, Tomato Egg Drop Soup, Preserved Sichuan Pickle And Sliced Pork Soup, Seafood Egg Drop Congee, Mushroom Chicken Congee, etc., sometimes make one wonder whether KFC is turning into a Chinese fast food chain. Therein lies the essence, and the success, of its product localization program.

Supply localization has been a focus of KFC China from day one, led by its QA and purchasing teams. A lot of hard work over many years by many KFC employees went into persuading, screening, and assisting foreign suppliers to set up local manufacturing capabilities in China. Even more hard work went into cultivating, educating, and enabling local Chinese suppliers to meet KFC's stringent product specifications.

In addition to food supplies, almost all hardware and service categories across the board have been localized. These supply localization efforts brought to KFC China not only significantly lower costs compared to imports, but also reduced risk of supply interruption due to uncontrollable factors such as inclement weather, shipment delays, labor strikes, and government-imposed import/export sanctions. The long-term benefits of these localization measures, including cost savings and favorable publicity, are enormous.

In the end, localization of employees, products, and supplies directly and indirectly – through a multiplying effect – stimulated the growth of the local economy, which in turn benefited local businesses, including KFC.

*   *   *

CONCLUSION

In China, KFC and McDonald's represent two different approaches to managing their respective businesses in terms of the profile of their local leadership team, product portfolio, brand positioning, advertising, and supply chain. In the end, these differences boil down to, fundamentally, a difference between a more localized approach versus a more global approach. While there is no one clear winning approach around the world, in China, it is clear that:

- Overall market characteristics are very different from other more established country markets in terms of history, language, culture, political system, economic system, and consumer characteristics;
- market diversity is high, and the speed of change is rapid, requiring both flexibility and speed of response; and
- market potential is huge, making the return on investment of localization programs more financially attractive.

Under these circumstances, more local adaptations to global standards, systems, processes, and procedures seem to be more effective.

Throughout its 20-year history, KFC China has demonstrated a surprising degree of flexibility, creativity, and willingness to adapt to the changing local environment. Compared to McDonald's, KFC's approach seems to be more effective based on results to date. As KFC and McDonald's continue to expand in China, what will be the key factors determining their future success? I cannot say for certain. What I do know is that the flexibility, creativity, and willingness to adapt that are inherent in KFC China's "personality" will continue to serve it well in the market environment of dynamic changes at high speed that is China.

10

HEADQUARTERS SUPPORT

INTRODUCTION

L ocal adaptations of corporate standard, policy, and management systems cannot take place without approval and support from corporate headquarters. On the other hand, corporate support does not mean the absence of corporate influence in the presence of local adaptations.

At the end of 2005, the China division, based largely on KFC's performance and, to a much lesser extent, Pizza Hut's performance, accounted for 14 percent of YUM! Brands' worldwide revenue and 16 percent of its worldwide operating margin. As a matter of fact, due to its growing importance, beginning in 2005 the China division reported directly to the CEO, David Novak, bypassing the international division.

David Novak's enthusiasm for China began long before 2005, when YUM! Brands was first spun off from PepsiCo back in 1997, and he was made the president under the tutelage of then-CEO Andy Pearson. From the beginning, Andy Pearson and David Novak shared an enthusiasm for KFC's long-term growth prospects in China. Their own actions spoke plenty about their enthusiasm. Each year since 1997, David Novak has visited China at least once. These visits are not merely intended to show his support for the increasingly important China operation. They also provide an opportunity for him and other visiting corporate officers to witness first hand the transformation of China, and KFC's as well as its competitors' operations in China, enriching their direct exposure to the local market conditions each time.

Corporate Support for Localization

It is impressive to see the degree of autonomy enjoyed by KFC compared to McDonald's in China, from new product development and introduction to new brand introduction; from distribution logistics to advertising and promotion; from restaurant operational procedures to franchisee selection procedures; the list goes on. Chapter 5 showed how KFC China, through the introduction of new products not available anywhere else around the world, slowly repositioned its brand image to an "American brand with Chinese characteristics." Similar autonomy is evidenced by KFC China's attempts at brand repositioning through TV advertising, public relations, and government relations programs. Under normal circumstances, most multinational corporations insist on individual country markets following global standards for product, advertising, and other business elements of brand positioning. McDonald's certainly does.

While examples abound in illustrating YUM! Brands corporate headquarters' support for various programs of localization, one example in particular illuminates the level of authority that has been delegated to KFC China. A few years ago, KFC China began testing a new brand concept called East Dawning in Shanghai. East Dawning is an experiment with Chinese fast food, the viability of which, in my opinion, is questionable. Not because the concept of Chinese fast food has been tried and failed many times around the world in recent decades. Rather, there are several fundamental, built-in conflicts between the nature of a QSR chain and the way the average Chinese consumer prefers his or her Chinese food served.

First, by definition a QSR chain must standardize on a limited menu for reasons related to operational efficiency, cost control, and quality consistency. Yet, Chinese consumers prefer a wide variety of dishes spread out on a dinner table when they go out for Chinese food.

Second, in order to be quick in service, a QSR must "manufacture to inventory" instead of "manufacture to order." Yet, Chinese consumers prefer their food served freshly prepared.

Third, traditional Chinese food preparation is a form of art, carried out by individual culinary artists with individual specialties and unique variations. When Chinese go out to eat Chinese food, they are driven by different specialties of different restaurants rather than the same food from the same restaurant chain.

Fourth, Chinese consumers have far more choices of different Chinese food than Western food and, therefore, are far more selective in choosing Chinese food. As a result, the market for Chinese food is far more competitive than the market for Western food in China. It's one thing to serve Chinese consumers Chinese food as a complement to American fried chicken; it's another to serve Chinese food, and only Chinese food, as a foreign restaurant chain competing against, literally, millions of other local restaurants offering authentic Chinese food that can be found on every street corner throughout China, especially in the absence of either a cost advantage or unique product differentiation.

My pessimistic assessment of the future of East Dawning aside, I nonetheless applaud the seemingly unreserved support from YUM! Brands for KFC China's propensity for risk-taking. In addition to a high level of tolerance for local adaptations and a strong willingness to delegate authority, support from YUM! Brands corporate headquarters for its China division comes in many other ways.

Corporate Support through Mission and Values

While YUM! Brands corporate headquarters delegated lots of authority to KFC China for local adaptation of systems and standards for restaurant operations, new product development, real estate development, and distribution and logistics, it has established corporate mission, values, systems, and processes – clear guidelines for all country operations, China included – to follow. These corporate values include respect for individual employees; employee recognition; "RGM #1"; "Customer Mania"; and so forth. Corporate systems and processes include CHAMPS, STAR, mystery shopper, competitive benchmarking, balanced scorecard, and 360-degree review.

Even those corporate systems and processes that have gone through extensive local customization in China have been extremely helpful because they provided a framework, thereby saving time and money by not having to start from scratch.

Corporate Support through Talents on Loan

Over the years, YUM! Brands has assigned the best-qualified functional talents drawn from all over the world to come to China's aid, each time for days, weeks, or years at a stretch. They cover a broad range of functions from finance and accounting to distribution/logistics, restaurant operation, and beyond. The frequency of exchange covering such a broad spectrum of functions over the years has brought increased communication, understanding, and bonding between the China division and various other KFC operations in the rest of the world.

Corporate Support through Timely Decision Making

Given KFC China's strategy based on aggressive and rapid restaurant expansion, speed of decision-making is a critical element in the successful implementation of this strategy. As can be expected, in the day-to-day operation of KFC in China, decisions of both a tactical and a strategic nature often require corporate approvals. Restaurant site screening and selection is a good example of a tactical decision requiring corporate approval during the 1990s. Sometimes, while waiting for corporate approval before the lease agreement for a proposed new KFC restaurant site can be signed, other prospective lessee(s), oftentimes direct competitors, are lurking in the wings, creating enormous time pressure. Based on my memory, not once did a required approval from the YUM! Brands headquarters hold up a new restaurant lease agreement.

Corporate Support through Public Praise and Recognition

In his Letter to the Shareholders in the 2004 Annual Report of YUM! Brands, David Novak, chairman and chief executive officer, laid out four different strategies to grow earnings per share at least 10 percent per year in future years. First on his list was "Build Dominant China Brands." He continued by saying that YUM! Brands already has two dominant brands in China, KFC and Pizza Hut, in their respective categories, quick service and casual dining. He went on to introduce Pizza Hut Home Delivery, Taco Bell Grande Dine-In, and East Dawning. He then concluded with a prediction that, one day, YUM! Brands will have more restaurants in China than in the United States. I think he is correct in making that prediction, but I think he may be surprised by the composition of YUM! Brands China's revenue and profit contribution by brand when that happens.

Clearly, Novak sees the China division as a growth engine for YUM! Brands in the decades ahead. He's right. By the end of 2010, China could account for a third or more of YUM! Brands' worldwide operating margin, and rising. Needless to say, Novak over the years has bestowed a countless number of accolades in various forms, in public and in private, upon the China division and the China team. Of them, the most telling is a term that has often appeared in his public addresses in recent years, a term he picked up during one of his first visits to China in the late 1990s. It's what he calls the YUM! "Dynasty." In the 2004 Annual Report, Novak continued:

"Going forward, we are galvanized around building what we call the YUM! Dynasty, driving consistent results year after year, which as you know, is the hallmark of truly great companies." Now, that is an appropriate and outstanding term of praise for its China division: *dynasty* – true to its origin!

Corporate Support through Benchmarking and Best Practice Sharing

Over the years, YUM! Brands has consistently been scouting for external and internal best practices, and spreading the best of these practices throughout the company. Two of these were put into practice in YUM! China during the late 1990s: the organizational effectiveness survey, and the functional audit. The former is usually an annual event, but can be conducted at more frequent intervals such as bi-annually or quarterly; the latter can be a one-time event on an as-needed basis or an annual event.

The organizational effectiveness survey is a voluntary, anonymous survey of employees. Each questionnaire is divided into 20 different sections, each with its own theme, including: customer focus, teamwork, customer service standard, results and accountability, communications, support for front line, coaching and support, belief in people, encouragement of risk taking, people development, reward and recognition, decision making, valuing difference, and career growth. Analyzing the survey results over time and by different segments – office locations and employee groups based on different salary grade levels, job functions, age, seniority, and education level – reveals meaningful data for management to act on in order to improve employee morale and organizational effectiveness over time. In service industries, high employee morale – especially among frontline employees – leads to improved customer service, enhanced customer satisfaction, repeat business, customer loyalty, and improved financial performance and competitive position over time.

Some people associate any functional audit with a negative connotation, based on the assumption that an audit is conducted only when something goes wrong. This is not the case. The type of functional audit at KFC China is a comprehensive, systematic, and objective analysis of a function's strengths and weaknesses aimed at the development of an action plan for further improvement. The underlying premise is based on the concept of continuous improvement.

Each functional audit follows a broad outline. The outline for marketing, for instance, can look like this:

I.   Market Environment Audit
  A. External factors
  B. Internal factors
II. Marketing Strategy Audit
  A. Mission
  B. Goals and objectives
  C. Strategy
III. Marketing Organization Audit
  A. Functional efficiency
  B. Interface efficiency
IV. Marketing Systems Audit
  A. Marketing planning system
  B. Marketing control system
  C. Product management system

V. Marketing Performance Audit
  A. Revenue
  B. Profitability
  C. Productivity and efficiency
VI. Marketing Function Audit
  A. Product
  B. Advertising
  C. Promotion
  D. Pricing
  E. Channel of distribution

CONCLUSION

Ironically, of all the contributions to the success of KFC China made by its corporate parent, none outweighs the importance of "leaving it alone." In other words, the most effective approach for the corporate parent to manage KFC China is to manage as little as possible, especially in its early days, when local conditions are varied, unclear and fast-changing; resources are tight; frequent "trials and errors" are necessary; and pressure for timely action is high. This observation, however, is based on a fundamental assumption that the local leadership team in place is the most qualified available. In the West, it's called delegation of authority and accountability. Come to think of it, should this not be the most effective approach to corporate management of a global enterprise under most circumstances anyway, especially in the situation of a fast-changing market environment in uncharted water? In such a "frontier" environment, the tried and proven approach often does not work, and the time for endless rounds of bottom-up reporting, internal review, reversed education, and layers of approval can be a prohibitively expensive, if not fatal, luxury.

Such was the environment that existed in China back in the 1980s and 1990s. Two different companies, KFC and McDonald's, chose two different paths when they were confronted with the same conditions found in China at the time. One decided to approach the market with a clean slate, an open mind, lots of flexibility, and a willingness to build a system from scratch that would match the local conditions. The other, long the most successful fast-food restaurant chain in the world, decided to import its successful model of operation, which had been proven effective in much of the rest of the world, into China.

During 2005 and 2006, a series of major organizational overhauls within McDonald's China took place, resulting in two company veterans being transferred from the U.S. to take over the helm. Are the latest actions of "headquarters support" the best solution for the challenges facing McDonald's China? Time will tell.

Same industry, two companies.

Two different corporate "personalities."

Two different interpretations, and manifestations, of "headquarters support." Two different sets of results to date.

Which approach to "headquarters support" do you prefer? I guess that depends, in part, on whether you're on the ground, or up in the tower, doesn't it?

11

LEADERSHIP WITH CHINESE CHARACTERISTICS

THE VISION THING

S am Su, president of YUM! Brands China, often says that one day, KFC will have 10,000 restaurants in China. In the words of two business strategy gurus, Gary Hamel and C.K. Prahalad, this is Sam's statement of strategic intent. Why 10,000? I never asked Sam, but I surmise it's for one or both of these reasons:

1. It's a big number, big enough to motivate employees of KFC China for a few decades to come. In the words of James Collins and Jerry Porras, authors of *Built To Last*, it's a "BHAG" – Big Hairy Audacious Goal.
2. Ten thousand happens to be a figure in between the number of KFC restaurants operating in the U.S. at the beginning of this century, and the number of McDonald's restaurants operating in the U.S. at the same time. Therefore, 10,000 is a convenient, round number with a ring of familiarity and authenticity to it.

Over the years, KFC China's senior leadership team has remained relatively stable. This is particularly amazing in a business environment where the average tenure for professional positions in a city like

Shanghai is less than three years. Causes for KFC's exceptional track record of leadership stability range from a competitive compensation system to a winning and positive work environment, tied to excellent financial performance and a rising brand. In addition, the personal influence and charisma of Sam Su cannot be ignored.

Born and raised in Taiwan, Sam rose through the merit-based and highly competitive education system of Taiwan, eventually graduating from the leading university there, the National Taiwan University, with a degree in chemical engineering. Like many of the best young talents from Taiwan in those days, Sam headed for America to pursue his graduate education in chemical engineering. Later, after receiving his MBA from Wharton, Sam spent a few years with Proctor & Gamble before joining PepsiCo in May 1989 as KFC's regional marketing director for the North Pacific and, later in the same year, concurrently as acting general manager of KFC China. At the time, KFC had four restaurant units operating in China. In 1997, when Tricon – which later became YUM! Brands – spun off from PepsiCo, Sam was appointed Tricon's head of Greater China. With first-hand experience and knowledge about both China and the West, Sam was uniquely qualified to lead KFC's rapid expansion in China.

BENEVOLENT DICTATORSHIP?

Over the years, I have heard statements from a number of sources suggesting that Sam's leadership style borders on the autocratic. Others disagree, myself included.

Politically, for over two millennia prior to the founding of the Chinese Republic in 1912, China had a long history of imperial dynasties when the emperor ruled with absolute power and authority with a "Mandate from the Heaven." For nearly as long, Chinese society operated in a highly hierarchical structure after Confucianism was first established as the state philosophy early in the Han Dynasty. Even after the founding of the republic, for over half a century China's political stage was dominated by two modern-day dictators: first, Chiang Kai-Shek; and later on, after 1949, Mao Tse-Dong. In other words, China has a very long history of strongman politics.

Chinese citizens, reflecting their larger social, cultural, and political reality, generally are not trained to be independent thinkers, nor direct and vocal advocates of their individual points of view, especially when facing figures of authority. On the other hand, over the years some local employees of KFC China have successfully immersed into KFC's company culture, gradually adjusting their behaviors to better conform with company values such as direct, open, and honest communication based on mutual trust and respect. In a market environment where the speed of decision-making and action implementation are key factors for business success, resulting in very little time for broad consensus building, Sam's determination, decisiveness, and lack of patience sometimes contributed to his image as a dictator. At other times, employees' deference to authority figures also contributed to the misunderstanding, and misrepresentation, of Sam's leadership style.

With that said, however, what matters the most is whether or not Sam's leadership style has worked for KFC China in the past, and more important, will it work in the future?

Support and Challenge Them

In my opinion, Sam qualifies for both repect and fondness. One of the ways Sam earns respect is with his ability to recognize, attract, challenge, motivate, and retain good talent with a knack for a flexible management style. Take myself, for example. Knowing that he can trust me with getting the most challenging projects completed without any close supervision, Sam offered me a long leash.

Shortly after joining YUM! Brands, I proposed to the Greater China Executive Committee, which Sam chaired, to consolidate and centralize all restaurant support functions, beginning with those under my direct responsibility – purchasing, QA, new product development, distribution and logistics, new market and real estate development, and IT. All members of the Executive Committee agreed that this was a necessary step before KFC China would be ready to move on to the next phase of restaurant expansion. Some worried about strong resistance from the field, especially from the joint venture markets. In the end, with Sam's support and approval, my proposal was completed far ahead of schedule, generating improved product quality, tens of millions of U.S. dollars of cost savings, improved organizational efficiency, and a solid platform for accelerated restaurant expansion.

While I appreciated Sam's long leash and respected him for the business results that KFC China has delivered under his leadership, many colleagues feared him. Why? First, Sam can be direct, persistent, and probing in asking pointed questions in internal meetings. At the same time, he is sharp, experienced, and knowledgeable. He has been in the same role since 1989 and knows everything that needs to be known about KFC China, as well as everyone in this business. When he asks questions, he expects a well-prepared, well thought-through response. Those who are well prepared and dare to take him on usually win his respect, while others who don't fare as well can end up receiving constructive feedback in public, losing "face" in the process. Second, Sam is tough, competitive, and determined. When push comes to shove, with his direct manner and style, Sam can seem intimidating to some, especially in front of deferential subordinates. Third, Sam sets ambitious targets and expects them to be achieved. Those on his team appearing to be less than competent or unwilling to try hard enough are relentlessly challenged to meet or exceed targets.

While Sam is performance-focused and results-driven, leadership traits that are not intrinsically Chinese, his leadership style includes many features of Chinese characteristics.

Protect Them

One of Sam's favorite field commanders developed a brain tumor in early 2000. Treatment in California brought the tumor under control, but not a full recovery. After returning from an initial surgical operation with a noticeable speech impediment, Sam put this person back into an important operational role. This person recently retired from KFC and was rewarded with a franchise for a new KFC restaurant in a big eastern Chinese city.

Watch Out For Local Warlords

Since the early 1990s, Sam has played a direct role in the recruitment and promotion of every single one of KFC China's market general managers, as well as key staff positions overseeing various functions in the Shanghai Restaurant Support Center. Over the years, Sam kept in close touch with them – especially the market general managers – even when they did not report to him directly, all for a good reason. Each market is like a cylinder in KFC China's engine of growth, and each market general manager is like a cylinder master, without whom the KFC China engine wouldn't run.

Every few years, Sam would rotate these market general managers to a different market in order to present them with a new and challenging experience, while at the same time guarding against field commanders becoming too deeply entrenched in their local turfs. A lesson that is, no doubt, gleaned from a few thousand years of imperial administration through the Chinese dynasties.

Give Them "Face"

The culture of YUM! Brands emphasizes employee recognition. Sam created the Dragon Award in order to recognize employees who have made a significant contribution to the success of KFC China. The award is usually given out at the annual YUM! China RGM conference. The choice of a dragon as the symbolic base for this much-coveted award is excellent, and it is such a natural choice to those familiar with Chinese history and culture. After all, how befitting for someone born in the year of the dragon (as Sam was), to present a Dragon Award to yet another dragon from the dragon dynasty of YUM Brands!

I sometimes wondered what symbol a non-Chinese general manager, such as Sam's counterpart at McDonald's during 2006, might have selected for the same award. Probably not a dragon, given the somewhat negative connotations associated with dragons in the West. To me this was simply another small example of the power of the "Taiwan Gang." Their understanding of China came so naturally, almost instinctively, in ways large and small, requiring no market studies, no climbing of any learning curves and, of course, no translation. The dragon, according to Chinese mythology, flies high at the top of the animal kingdom and, for centuries, has been a symbol of the emperor. A Dragon Award connotes exclusiveness, excellence, and prestige, playing very well to the Chinese concept of "face."

The Chinese concept of "face" connotes respect and recognition from the "face giver"; pride and joy from the "face recipient." "Face" can be positive (gaining face) or negative (losing face). Thus, when a KFC China employee receives a Dragon Award in public, he or she is "gaining face." On the other hand, when a KFC China employee is caught accepting bribes from a supplier, then both the employee and the companies are "losing face."

In the absence of formal religions, the concept of "face," which is based on the precepts of pride, shame, and public opinion, becomes an important substitute for moral principles. It is interesting to note that Hu Jin-Tao, current chairman of the CCP, initiated a new public campaign dubbed "Eight Prides, Eight Shames" in March 2006 as part of an effort to create a "Harmonious Society," reminiscent of various elements of Confucianism. Is China, after nearly three decades of blinding materialistic pursuit and six decades of near-total abandonment of Confucian values, finally ready to return to its cultural roots once again?

Of Company and Family

Roger and Elaine, the two Taiwanese professionals weighing the pros and cons of working in China in Chapter 2, present yet another example of Sam's leadership style with Chinese characteristics. Many multinational companies around the world prohibit married couples from working in the same department, the same division, or the same company. Sam's opinion during those pioneering days in the mid-1990s, when experienced industry veterans were in high demand, was that any potential risk or discomfort stemming from their married status was far outweighed by the benefit of their talents. Furthermore, both contributed significantly to KFC China's success.

Therefore, Sam concluded NOT to initiate any action that would change the employment status of Roger and Elaine, or other married couples in similar circumstances. These were not easy decisions. Couples in senior positions working from the same office, albeit in different functions, do run into awkward situations between themselves, among peers, and especially with their subordinates. Sam made a difficult decision after considering the pros and cons. As a professional manager, I cannot say that I agreed with Sam's decision.

Nevertheless, I respected Sam for his courage, conviction, and determination with which he made this and other decisions.

Over the years, of those reporting directly to Sam, not many chose to leave the company. For those who might have contemplated leaving, Sam would try his very best to convince them to stay. Before resigning from KFC for another much smaller company experiencing big problems near the end of 2000, I gave Sam several months' notice. Sam tried to convince me to stay, offering me other job opportunities in Asia and in the U.S. While Sam did this, no doubt, out of loyalty and obligation to YUM! Brands, as well as personal interest, he made me feel that he was approaching the issue as a friend, or even as a family member, rather than a colleague, which is very typical of Sam's leadership style.

Sam's paternalistic way of treating members of his "inner circle" – those who have contributed to the success of KFC China – earned him fierce personal loyalty in return. In more ways than one, if you have proven yourself and earned your place, Sam, as head of the family, will look after your best interests and protect you in times of need.

Sources of Paternalism

Traces of paternalistic patterns in Chinese business leadership behavior can be traced to the very depths of Confucianism, beginning with the concept of "Mandate of Heaven." Under an unspoken contract between the emperor and his subordinates, as long as the emperor remains a benevolent ruler, the emperor retains absolute authority over those being ruled. Other Confucian concepts, such as *Qing* and *Yi*, also serve to strengthen paternalistic values and behaviors.

The Confucian concept of *Yi*, which can be translated into "loyalty," "chivalry," "justice," or "righteousness," has, in fact, much broader implications. At the very least, the concept of *Yi* connotes mutual moral obligations between two individuals or within a group of individuals. A good example of *Yi* is the brotherhood exemplified in the Chinese classic *All Men Are Brothers* written by Shih Naian of the Yuan Dynasty (1279–1368 AD), who wrote about a period in the Song Dynasty during the first half of the twelfth century when 108 men and women united together under a "Big Brother" to rebel against oppressive and corrupt government officials. Another quintessential illustration of the concept of *Yi* is presented through a historic novel, *The Three Kingdoms*, written by Luo Guangzhong of the Ming Dynasty (1368–1644 AD) about a much earlier period in the second and the third century AD during which three men were bonded in a life-and-death brotherhood in their collective pursuit of victory and glory. Both novels, like their closest Western counterpart, *Robin Hood*, revolve around the concept of *Yi*, loyalty of brotherhood among men of honor.

On the surface, the Chinese concept of *Qing* means feelings, emotions, or sentiments. In this case, we can refer to *Ren-Qing,* which can be translated into favors asked, owed, or given, or goodwill expressed in the form of a gift, an invitation to a meal, or other friendly gestures. So, if your friend does you a favor, you owe him *Ren-Qing*. If you are a gentleman, you should some day return his *Ren-Qing*. Central to the concept of *Ren-Qing* is the notion of reciprocity. You will note that the concept of *guanxi* discussed previously is related, at least remotely, to the concept of *Ren-Qing*. To maintain good *guanxi*, one must, among other things, first take good care of *Ren-Qing*.

Both of these concepts, *Qing* and *Yi*, play an important role in the interactions among ethnic Chinese raised with traditional Chinese values like Sam and other members of KFC's "Taiwan Gang."

Risks of Paternalism

While a paternalistic leadership style fosters a close-knit leadership team with minimum loss of talents and associated organizational disruptions, it is not without risks and costs. What is its impact on future generations of leadership within the organization, especially on those who are not, or not yet, the accepted members of the "family"? What is its impact on building a meritocracy-centered company culture? What will happen when the head of the family exits from the stage? Can paternalism co-exist with fairness, equity, and transparency? Is it good for shareholders and other stakeholders? These are controversial questions.

Is there a correct, or most effective, approach to leadership in China? The answer, of course, is no. It's situation-dependent, as is the case everywhere else around the world. At the macro level, it depends, at least in part, on the evolution of the Chinese economy and the extent of its globalization. As long as the Chinese economy continues to be more or less closed to the world outside, with the government playing an active role, old ways of doing business based on *guanxi* and paternalistic values will continue to prevail. We know, however, that this is not the case.

Today, China continues to move forward in alignment with global mainstream business values and practices, however slowly. En route, the Chinese economic system will have to adopt the most economically efficient approach in order to be competitive on the global stage. Meritocracy makes the most business sense because it encourages and allows the best talents in an organization to advance based upon results and performance rather than personal relationships and origins of birth. As long as China continues its current course of economic reforms and global integration, the Chinese economy is likely to edge closer to a merit-based system over time, purely out of competitive necessity. However, it might take generations.

DEVELOPING FUTURE GENERATIONS OF LEADERSHIP

The future of KFC China will not be in the hands of Sam Su or, for that matter, any other member of the "Taiwan Gang." The future of KFC China will be in the hands of current, as well as future, generations of local Chinese. What motivates them?

In more ways than one, the average up-and-coming local Chinese managers employed by KFC are motivated by the same factors as their peers around the world – income, promotion, recognition, upward mobility and interesting and challenging job opportunities. One factor does set them apart from their contemporaries elsewhere, and that is the value they place on employer-provided training. In part designed to address this employee expectation, but also to meet the demand presented by extremely rapid growth in the number of restaurants, KFC China invested sizeable high-quality resources into employee training and development at all levels early on.

For a variety of reasons including language differences, speed of restaurant growth, and scale efficiency, KFC China developed its own educational infrastructure instead of relying on YUM! Brands' global and regional infrastructures and tools for employee education. Experienced restaurant managers and administrators were brought together to build this important function from scratch. A training and development center was established in Shanghai. Field managers, as part of their career development, were rotated through the training center as teachers and facilitators so that students could better relate to their real-life, hands-on restaurant operational experience. These field managers also contributed to the assembly, as well as the revision, of teaching materials that reflected real and current field issues, problems, challenges, and opportunities.

Over the years, this training system that was built for, and managed by, restaurant operations produced generations of future KFC China restaurant operation leaders. At the same time, this training system continued with its own self-renewal process through program reformatting, content upgrading, and personnel exchanges between the field and the Shanghai headquarters. In the process, it became a practical and cost-effective way to train, motivate, and retain a continuous supply of well-trained restaurant management talents. Of those who participated in this training system and later left KFC, many went on to spread the knowledge they acquired while being trained by KFC, further contributing to the improvement of the restaurant service industry in China to the ultimate benefit of all Chinese consumers.

In addition to broadly based formal training and development programs available to all rising local stars, KFC China relies on other methods to train, develop, recognize, and reward its most valuable talents. These methods include company-sponsored opportunities to pursue education in business administration and temporary assignments – sometimes overseas assignments, which are highly sought-after by local Chinese employees.

As a side note, the roots of the Chinese penchant for education run deep into the culture, and start early in life. The daughter of my one-time assistant at KFC recently graduated from an EMBA Program in Shanghai. At the time of graduation, Stephanie was six years old. The program is two years in duration, targets children three to six years of age, and costs US$3,000, not an insignificant sum even for a senior-middle level manager working for an American company in Shanghai. "E" stands for early.

Mentoring

In 1999, sensing a growing discontent among the highest-ranking local Chinese employees over the lack of upward mobility, I began advocating for a mentoring program. Each member of the Greater China Executive Committee was assigned a few of the most promising middle and senior-middle managers to coach, counsel, and assist in their individual career planning and development over and beyond the normal HR processes.

Most of these rising young talents carried the title of director or senior manager. Zheng Gang was one of those assigned to me, and I was delighted to be able to work with him. As the head of real estate development for KFC's Beijing market, Zheng Gang had a very important mission then, which was to overtake McDonald's as the market leader in Beijing. As Zheng Gang's assigned mentor, I had a responsibility to work with him on the development of his career plan, and to look after his best career interests. I once approached him about a two-year assignment in KFC China's Shanghai headquarters as part of his long-term career development. In the end, he declined because he and his team were getting very close to overtaking McDonald's Beijing and he wanted to be there when the moment of triumph arrived. I respected his decision, and left it at that after Zheng Gang promised he would reconsider relocating to Shanghai after KFC overtook McDonald's in Beijing. It happened within a year after I left. Recently, I heard Zheng Gang is now working in the Shanghai Restaurant Support Center.

Another one of the local Chinese managers whom I personally mentored in the absence of a mentor program was Garrison Chu Lien-Sheng. Garrison was the head of QA in the Shanghai Restaurant Support Center, an important staff function. Even in those early days, Garrison struck me as very different from the rest of the local employees. He not only had a sharp and analytical mind, he was also down to earth and outspoken. Furthermore, he had a high sense of integrity. In addition, Garrison had many qualities of an effective business leader. He was confident, yet humble. He worked hard, and delivered results. He was decisive. His subordinates respected him, as did his peers and superiors.

The more I observed Garrison, the more I felt that it was my duty to pay special attention to his career development. After obtaining concurrence from Garrison's immediate superior, the three of us began a discussion about Garrison's future career plan. Pretty soon we came to the conclusion that in order to realize his career goal of becoming a general manager, Garrison needed to move into a restaurant operations role, which was a very different function from where he'd spent his career up to that point, managing suppliers and products instead of managing restaurants.

A transfer from QA into restaurant operations would require many months, even years, of learning how to run a restaurant from the ground level up. It was a risky proposition, giving up a strong career track in QA to move into an unfamiliar role within restaurant operations, stepping back from a senior-level position to engage in an entry-level position in the process, a "face-losing" proposition. Garrison was very willing to take the risk, and I did not discourage him because I knew, deep down, he wanted to do it, and YUM! Brands would benefit from this development transfer in the long run. It took me a while to convince Garrison's immediate superior to let go of the most valuable contributor within his department, and that this move would be in Garrison's, as well as KFC's, best long-term interest. Eventually, Garrison was put on a Pizza Hut restaurant operation management development track. I was convinced Garrison had made a wise, long-term career decision, and was very happy for him, as well as for YUM!

When I first learned in early 2004 that Garrison had left KFC to become the general manager of Papa John's (pizza restaurant chain) in Shanghai, I had very mixed feelings. On one hand, I was happy for Garrison, as he'd achieved his career goal of becoming a general manager. On the other hand, it was a loss for KFC, and I had to wonder to myself, how many more Garrisons will there be? I have little doubt that KFC China has an expansive talent pool to replace the Garrisons of the world. Perhaps Garrison's exit is simply unavoidable when an organization grows to be so big. Still, I can't help but wonder, how can the risk of losing precious talents be minimized, even for aspiring monoliths like KFC China?

Succession

Sam Su is a capable general manager. His knowledge about the QSR industry in China is both broad and deep. His direct involvement in

KFC China dates back to the late 1980s. Most members of his senior staff readily pledge their personal allegiance to him. Given these facts, it is not surprising that Sam has had a strong hold on the helm of KFC China for a long time. Under these circumstances, despite efforts by Sam and other members of KFC's senior leadership team to grow, develop, and expand the bench, one haunting question that's in the back of many observers' mind is who will succeed Sam, and when? Will the flame of KFC China's success be carried forward long after Sam's exit from the stage, which is, after all, the true lasting mark of an effective leadership?

Whoever succeeds Sam will most likely be unable to enjoy the same level of command and respect from employees, suppliers, and partners. In fact, his successor may well bring a very different style of leadership, which might be just as appropriate for the next phase of KFC's growth in China. This new leadership style may be more nurturing and sympathetic to consensus building; more willing to share power and influence and to delegate; more open to a decentralized organizational structure; more tolerant of different points of view; and more amenable to peaceful resolutions over differences with suppliers, franchisees, and joint venture partners.

Perhaps the question of who will succeed Sam is not that important, as his successor will surely be surrounded and supported by a strong team of talents and plenty other resources. In any event, I hope that person will have the courage to develop his of her own path of leadership instead of imitating his/her predecessor's. As well as I know Sam, I am confident that he will have the wisdom and the self-discipline to make room, and to cheer on the sideline, for his own successor, and generations of future KFC China leadership, when the time comes.

CONCLUSION

Even a strong leader such as Sam Su could not have built KFC China without a strong team – a team with strong skill sets and stronger still commitment to achieve industry leadership against improbable odds. Through the collective hard work of a stable senior leadership team working together over many years, a strong KFC China company culture emerged. Part of it derives from YUM! Brands' corporate values, including values placed on employee recognition and a healthy regard for restaurant operation staff. Other values are more local in origin, including KFC China's paternalistic way of treating senior-level employees who have made significant contributions, and their corresponding company loyalty to KFC China and personal loyalty to Sam Su.

While one can argue about the appropriate mix of local values, policies, and even exceptions within a multinational corporation, few can discount the strength, stability, and cohesiveness of the first-generation KFC China leadership team. Fewer still can disregard the spectacular success, as measured in revenue and profit growth, relative market share, competitive advantage, and brand recognition this first-generation leadership team, led by Sam Su, has achieved.

12

PAST AND FUTURE

THE PAST

B y any account, the story of KFC China to date has been a story of immense success. In 20 years it has grown from zero to 2,000 restaurants with an average restaurant profit margin of 20 percent, becoming the leading restaurant chain in China. Its archrival around the world, McDonald's, pales by a significant margin in terms of size, growth, and profitability. Internally, KFC China is the fastest growing, and the most profitable, division within its corporate parent company, YUM! Brands.

The theme of this book revolves around this question: what factors contributed to KFC's success in China? To address this question, we must first develop an appreciation for the complexity and the dynamism behind the modern-day Chinese economy, Chinese consumers, and their historical and cultural roots. (*Chapter 1*) Only when the complex and dynamic nature of China, its people, and its history are understood can readers better appreciate the relevance of each of the key factors behind KFC's success in China, including:

A leadership team endowed with a deep understanding of this market environment and its historical roots, years of industry experience accumulated in other more mature Asian QSR markets, and an abundance of entrepreneurial drive, energy, innovativeness, and flexibility. (*Chapter 2*)

Next, a business strategy built around the scale and speed of market expansion, first by establishing major market hubs up and down China's eastern coast, later by filling in the space between these hubs with a rising density of restaurants while expanding westward to China's interiors. (*Chapter 3*)

Other factors critical to KFC China's success include various elements required in the successful implementation of its strategy built around speed, scale, flexibility, innovation, and efficiency:

- When joint venture was the only viable alternative in the late 1980s and early 1990s, KFC selected local partners with government connections and effectively leveraged their tangible and intangible local resources. Once joint ventures were no longer required by Chinese regulations, and sufficient learnings and resources had been transferred from the local partners, KFC went direct in order to avoid the paralysis that can result from disagreements between partners, and expanded aggressively. (*Chapter 4*)
- Understand the target customers, and localize the total product offerings to meet customers' needs, from food and-dining environment to service. Develop an American brand image with Chinese characteristics. (*Chapter 5*)
- Build a local supply chain with total control over distribution and logistics, dedicated to serving KFC's restaurant expansion strategy anywhere, any time, at competitive cost and lightning speed. (*Chapter 6*)
- Develop a locally validated real estate management process with high forecasting accuracy to maximize the probability of success of each new market and new restaurant opened. (*Chapter 7*)
- Develop a highly effective human resource management system and restaurant operation management system to recruit, train, and develop restaurant employees in order to meet the high volume demand for restaurant management staff and to deliver superior products and service to customers. (*Chapter 8*)

- Localize. Custom-tailor organizational structure, management systems, processes, policies, people, and other internal and external resources to China's unique context. Adjust and invent new ones in anticipation of quantum change in a fast-moving environment. (*Chapter 9*)
- Turn corporate headquarters into a force of leverage and support, not hindrance. (*Chapter 10*)
- Lead with courage, determination, and a style that blends with the local context. Business success is built on the quality and the speed of decisions and actions over time, and begins with an experienced leadership team with an intrinsic knowledge of the local context. (*Chapter 11*)

Exhibit 14: Key Factors Behind KFC's Success in China

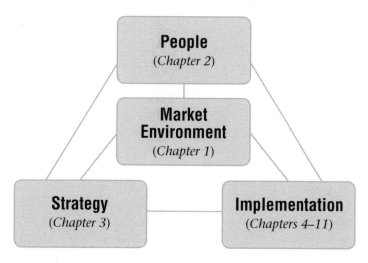

Formulating and Executing a Coherent Strategy

As Exhibit 14 illustrates, the connectivity among market context (*Chapter 1*), KFC China's leadership team (*Chapter 2*), their business strategy (*Chapter 3*), and various components for the strategy's successful implementation (*Chapters 4–11*) are just as important as, if not more than, each individual element. Standing alone, none of these four elements – context, people, strategy, and execution – can make KFC a success in China. Together, they jell, complement, and reinforce each other, producing wonderful – almost magical – business results. It is not the early establishment of major growth hubs throughout China, the captive logistics network, or, the various measures of localization of product, supply, employee, etc. that made the difference. Rather, it's all of them and more, linked together, complementing and reinforcing each other, that created a sustainable competitive advantage virtually impossible for any competitor to duplicate.

In summary, this is how people, strategy, and effective implementation worked together, and produced magic, for KFC in China:

1. An effective business strategy can only be designed based on deep knowledge of the local context. In other words, strategy is context-dependent. A strategy that works well in a stable and mature market economy would most likely not work well in China, given the diversity of its people and geography, the heritage of a rich and complex culture, and a rapidly and continuously changing business environment since China's economic reforms commenced in 1978.

2. Deep knowledge of the local context comes best from the best available local talents. In their absence, find the best substitutes. Through the 1990s, the best substitutes were the best available talents from Taiwan, based on which KFC assembled its initial China leadership team.

3. In the restaurant industry, economy of scale provides the basis for a sustainable competitive advantage until a point of diminishing return is reached. Until then, whoever leads in scale enjoys a tangible cost advantage as well as an intangible benefit of "face" or brand recognition. The combination of early entry, speedy expansion, and widening gap in scale has brought KFC increasing competitive advantage vis-à-vis its competitors in China.

4. The proof of the pudding lies in implementation. In China, successful implementation requires not only sound, localized products, people, systems, and processes, but also, and more importantly, flexibility and the ability to respond to change rapidly – the ability to change direction according to a new government policy, crisis, or opportunity. Better

yet, an ability to project forthcoming changes such as a new government policy, and to position your company's resources in anticipation accordingly.

Throughout its history in China, KFC has demonstrated time and again its ability to anticipate, and quickly adapt to, changes taking place in both the external and the internal environment. However, past achievements do not guarantee future success. What lies ahead for KFC China? What are the new challenges and opportunities? What changes in the external environment are likely to take place, which will affect KFC's future? What strategic revisions and new action programs are called for?

A PREMISE FOR THE FUTURE

These questions and predictions are based on a single, all-important assumption, which is that China's economy will grow at the rate of 7–10 percent per annum through 2025. There will always be some economists who prefer a doomsday view about the future of China and its economy. But today's mainstream economic community around the world shares a growing optimistic outlook that, barring some unforeseen worldwide calamity of an unpredictable nature, or a regional military flare-up involving China, the most likely of which would be over the issue of Taiwan's independence, China's GDP growth will continue at the rate of 7 percent or more per annum for at least another decade or two.

Under this broad scenario of continuing economic growth, what are the likely challenges facing future generations of KFC China's leadership team?

The Curse of Growth

The first challenge facing future generations of KFC China's leadership team is the rising expectation for KFC China's future growth based on recent success. Straightforward arithmetic would suggest that the exceptionally high growth rate will not continue forever.

Let's assume KFC China had 600 restaurants at the end of 2001, which is a close enough approximation. To add another 200 restaurants in 2002 – a good job, given the growth bottlenecks described in Chapter 3 – would have resulted in an annual growth rate of 33 percent. The same number of new restaurants, 200, would result in annual growth rate of 25 percent in 2003, 20 percent in 2004, declining to 10 percent in 2009, and a single-digit growth rate thereafter. Putting it another way, while 33 percent growth in 2002 meant 200 new restaurants for that year, 33 percent growth in 2009 would mean a bigger number of new restaurants. This growth curse can only get worse as the number of restaurants continues to rise from year to year. It's a no-win game, unless the growth rate is adjusted lower, which is not likely to happen, as KFC China has become the star of YUM! Brands' worldwide growth engine. As a matter of fact, the target for YUM! Brands China's growth rate in the foreseeable future has been set at 22 percent per year.

The challenge described above, which is inherent within any growing business, forces YUM! Brands China to search for additional sources of growth, most notably additional brands, of which YUM! Brands has a few. They include Pizza Hut, a casual dining concept already doing very well in China; Pizza Hut Express, which is China's version of Domino's Pizza (i.e. pizza home delivery service); Taco Bell; A&W; Long John Silver's; and East Dawning. Of them, KFC, Pizza Hut, and Pizza Hut Express have demonstrated strong potential in the China market and will remain strong contributors to YUM! Brands' future growth in China. However, KFC, Pizza Hut, and Pizza Hut Express put together will not be able to sustain the current targeted growth rate of 22 percent per annum for YUM! Brands China indefinitely, even after the doors to franchising KFC, Pizza Hut, and Pizza Hut Express are nudged wide open. Therefore, in order to maintain 22 percent revenue growth, the emergence in China of one or more of YUM! Brands' other brands will be increasingly needed in the coming decade, or sooner if East Dawning turns out not to be a spectacular success.

What is the prospect of another spectacular success among A&W, East Dawning, Long John Silver's, and Taco Bell in China? My personal assessment is that none of them will be able to approach the level of success of Pizza Hut, let alone KFC.

In Chapter 10, I explained why I don't think East Dawning will be a success in China. This is not to say the concept of a fast-food chain serving Chinese food in China will not take off. It might. If it does, it most likely will be a niche play catering to select urban market segments by serving a narrow range of unique, good-tasting Chinese food, not a broad sample of popular Chinese dishes. Besides, Chinese food is not the strength of KFC or, for that matter, YUM! Brands. Speed and convenience alone will not provide East Dawning with sufficient competitive differentiation against Chinese food already being offered in China with a broad range of flavors, quality, price, variety, and channels; nor will heavy advertising spending and brand tie-in with KFC. On the other hand, while the prospect of East Dawning does not appear encouraging in China, it may become a big sell outside China, an opportunity YUM! Brands should pursue actively and immediately.

Could future growth in China come from A&W, Long John Silver's, and Taco Bell? Not likely, given the nature of their core product offerings, Chinese consumer preferences, and competitive dynamics. Its failure in the Beijing market and the resulting tarnished reputation aside, A&W's core product offerings, including the hot dog and the root beer, do not stir up too much excitement in the taste bud of the average Chinese consumer. Long John Silver's way of preparing seafood is just not the same as a plate of deep-fried flounder or lightly-steamed rock cod, whole – with the head, tail, bones and the whole nine yard. Of the three, Taco Bell holds the most promise, but not if YUM! Brands continues to position it as a high-end, exotic dining concept (as it did, prior to closure, in Shanghai), nor if it continues to be beef-based. Pork maybe, but not beef, as McDonald's experience thus far in China has clearly demonstrated.

While KFC, Pizza Hut, and Pizza Hut Express continue to grow with a few hundred new restaurants in China through direct investment from YUM! Brands in the foreseeable future, current expectation to grow China division's revenue by 22 percent a year is not realistic, not even when aided by the RMB's continuing appreciation beyond 2010. This is particularly the case if earlier assessment of the prospect of A&W, East Dawning, Long John Silver's, and Taco Bell in China is correct. In that case, the percentage growth shortfall may start appearing as early as the first half of the coming decade.

This is why YUM! Brands may be forced to open the gate for faster, more aggressive franchising of KFC, Pizza Hut, and Pizza Hut Express, three proven main engines for YUM!'s growth in China in the foreseeable future. That will bring immediate relief to the pressure brought on by the target annual growth rate of 22 percent, but might trigger challenges of a different, perhaps more serious, nature – of tarnished brand image and stretched management resources. In any event, maintaining a growth rate of 20 percent or more in China becomes a growing challenge no matter how you look at it, as the restaurant base continues to grow.

The Challenge of Size

The second set of emerging challenges, both internal and external, come with growing size. Externally, as KFC's relative market share and brand presence continue to expand, politically controversial topics such as the green food movement, children's obesity linked to fast food, part-time wage levels, and employee unions will continue to demand a public response. So will many uncontrollable events such as recent negative publicity surrounding the red-dye incident and avian flu. Internally, as new restaurants, employees, and products continue to be brought on-line in great mass, the probability of product defects and employee judgment errors may rise in proportion.

The Challenge of Hubris and Arrogance

In the foreseeable future, the biggest threat facing KFC China will be KFC itself. Beyond that, anything is possible, given the dynamic and unpredictable nature of China's economy and politics. Despite the widening gap between KFC and McDonald's, history has shown that in a highly dynamic environment such as China, a few short years can make a huge difference. Arrogance derived from success can take many different forms, all the way from slow action to inaction; from a sense of invincibility and underestimating existing or potential competitive forces to being weighed down by a growing bureaucracy.

TRENDS AFFECTING KFC'S FUTURE IN CHINA

What should KFC do to effectively address these challenges? Before answering this question, let's first try to make an intelligent guess about the future of the market context in the next decade and beyond.

First, China will continue to exhibit the characteristics of uneven economic development and wealth distribution across different regions. While continuing economic growth will lift the standard of living of all Chinese citizens, the urban-rural divide will get worse before it gets better.

Second, as China's central government takes action in the next few decades to alleviate extreme poverty in the countryside by building roads, health clinics, electricity generators, and so on, new opportunities will emerge for KFC to continue its rapid expansion in rural China.

Third, rural to urban migration will continue in the coming decade, expanding KFC's potential customer base in urban centers. The combination of an expanding customer base and rising consumer income in urban population centers leaves room for continuing expansion even in "mature" markets.

Fourth, as Chinese economic planners place increasing emphasis on domestic consumption over exports and investments as the primary engine for economic growth, and introduce government policies to encourage private consumption in the years ahead, KFC and other consumer goods companies will benefit from this shift in government policy, in both urban and rural China.

Fifth, in line with overall economic development and the rising standard of living of the average Chinese consumer, consumer expectation will rise and multiply, further advancing a movement toward a pluralized society with diversified consumer tastes and preferences. These trends should benefit KFC China, given its innovative and flexible past, and assuming it will not be bogged down by a growing bureaucracy in the future.

Sixth, as China' economic structure shifts even more from public to private enterprises, and as China completes the process of alignment with the mainstream global trading community through the WTO, the role of government policy, guidance, and intervention in the business community may diminish, leaving more room for market forces and open competition, conditions that will benefit the fittest.

Seventh, the focus of the Chinese central government's economic policy will undergo a shift from quantity to quality with greater emphasis on environmental protection, efficient utilization of resources, social welfare, and other advanced economic and social causes in the next few decades. So will the basis for performance evaluation of government officials at various levels.

Eighth, as China's one-child policy comes under increasing internal scrutiny, pressure for loosening up will rise, prompting the Chinese central government to take actions. This, in turn, will have broad ramifications for KFC and other business enterprises throughout China for decades to come.

Ninth, while the RMB's controlled appreciation may continue beyond 2010, it is just a matter of time until the currency reaches a state of free float. When that happens, KFC China will not only lose a currency conversion bonanza, but it will also be subjected to unpredictable conversion risks up or down, creating far greater earnings volatility for KFC China and, consequently, for YUM! Brands.

One thing is certain: as the Chinese economy continues to grow at a high speed in the next twenty years, this economic growth will continue to drive changes in consumer values and behaviors, social structure, and regional developments as it has during the past twenty years. In the process, what used to work in the past is no guarantee that it will work, or work as well, in the future. In fact, it probably won't.

IMPACT OF FUTURE TRENDS ON PAST KEY SUCCESS FACTORS

1. **Leadership Team.** While the "Taiwan Gang" played its historical mission exceptionally well during the first two decades, it's time for the baton to be passed on to the local Chinese, not for any altruistic reasons, but simply because the locals understand this market even better than the "Taiwan Gang." Furthermore, while the locals were not experienced in the QSR industry nor well-inculcated in Western business values and protocols back in the 1980s and 1990s, they are

today. And they are ready. They are ready to take on the leadership challenge of the highest order, if they are allowed.

2. **Business Strategy.** While rapid accumulation of size and scale continues to make sense as KFC China's fundamental strategy in the foreseeable future, operational implications of its implementation from supply chain to brand management can differ a lot from the past. After all, assimilating new employees and new suppliers when hundreds of new restaurants are being opened across China each year, many in rural, third and fourth-tier cities, is not a simple or easy task. In any event, economic efficiency and brand efficiency must be supplemented by consumer perception of superior price performance and quality of food, service, and usage experience, which is some-times assigned only secondary priority when a company's focus is placed on meeting growth and earnings targets.

Going forward, KFC China should place as much emphasis on safeguarding its hard-earned brand reputation through maximizing product price performance and quality – of employees, products, suppliers, and all other elements necessary to deliver customer satis-faction – as financial metrics.

3. **Local Partnerships, Government Relations, and Public Relations.** While China steams ahead to a market economy, the prac-tical value of local partnerships established during the 1980s and the first half of the 1990s has eroded. In the coming years, KFC will face some tough decisions on whether, and how, to terminate decade(s)-long partnerships with joint venture and franchisee partners. If mishandled, termination of these partnerships will have significant financial, as well as public relations, implications. Likewise, as KFC grows in size and recognition, publicity becomes a sharper, double-edged sword that can cut both ways. Between government relations and press relations, KFC should gradually increase its emphasis on the latter as the Chinese government slowly moves away from its traditional activist role.

Contingency planning should shift more to emerging issues such as environmental protection, waste disposal, workers' rights and workers' unions, imbalance of labor supply across regions, rising cost of labor, and prices in general.

4. **Product and Marketing.** Product flavor, quality, and variety will continue to play a critical role in urban Chinese consumers' dine-out decisions, as will service, convenience, and speed. Rural Chinese consumers will continue to be attracted by the "exotic" nature of KFC in the coming decade. In the foreseeable future, KFC will face increasingly diverse target market segments, requiring a more sophisticated segmentation approach in response. For example, in the future KFC will no longer face the duality of urban versus rural China, but instead it will face the addition of suburban China and other emerging categories in market segmentation. Within each category, much more refined market segmentation based on demographic as well as psychographic dimensions will be needed.

On product strategy, while innovation, speed, and frequency of new product introductions will continue to be an attraction to the fashion-conscious youth segment, more attention in the future should be paid to the flavor, quality, and price performance of new products. Consistent and superior product flavor, good product quality, and attractive price performance – not the frequency of new product introduction – will be the most critical product drivers behind KFC's future success in China as consumer preference matures, consumer choices multiply, and competition intensifies.

Exceedingly frequent introduction of new products can detract consumer focus away from the core product offerings, sometimes even causing consumer confusion; create distractions among key suppliers, perhaps to the detriment of the quality of core products; and create quality risks among the workforce, both on the front-line and in the back-room. Instead of focusing on the variety and frequency of new product introductions, KFC should focus on product quality and price performance first.

5. **Supply Chain, Distribution, and Logistics.** At the end of 2005, China had over 40,000 kilometers of expressways, more than half of which were added during the previous five years. A decade before that, China had almost none. To put these figures in perspective, the United States had some 90,000 kilometers of expressways in 2005. By 2010, China's goal is to reach 65,000 kilometers, connecting all provincial capitals and cities with at least half a million residents, as well as many more with populations of at least two hundred thousand. At that point, China's expressway network will have reached

the standard of a select group of developed economies. Under such circumstances, KFC's competitive differentiator built on a captive warehouse and logistics system will increasingly become more of a financial liability than an asset, due primarily to the absence of back-hauling of delivery trucks. In other words, while KFC China's early decision was correct to build a captive logistics system in an environment of inadequate road infrastructure and the absence of third-party trucking and warehousing service providers, such is no longer the case today. Changes including an expanding expressway system and the emergence of world-class, third-party logistics service providers with nation-wide capabilities will increasingly call for the consideration of a strategy reversal.

As to the supply chain, KFC should continue the policy of keeping only a few suppliers for each SKU in order to optimize scale economy. However, to meet growing volume demand, instead of adding capacity to existing plant(s), KFC should urge suppliers to build new plants located in multiple locations throughout different parts of China in order to reduce transportation cost and single-factory risk while still benefiting from volume and management efficiencies.

6. **Real Estate Development.** While KFC should continue its expansion strategy with a pioneering attitude (i.e. to be the first Western fast-food chain restaurant to enter every Chinese city, township, or even village), the question of "how" merits careful periodic review. For example, should KFC consider a far more aggressive push for franchising in China, even more aggressive than what was announced in April of 2006, when the one-time entry fee was reduced by as much as 75 percent from the previous US$1 million? Should KFC consider a single real estate development team to cover KFC, Pizza Hut, Pizza Hut Express, and East Dawning's real estate development needs? Should KFC design smaller restaurants requiring less financial investment to cater to the needs of rural China? Should YUM! Brands China begin active experimentation with multi-branding – KFC and Taco Bell? Pizza Hut and Taco Bell?

7. **Restaurant Operation.** While CHAMPS remains the rallying point for maintaining restaurant operational excellence, strictest adherence to the highest operating standard needs to be sewn into

KFC China's company culture. Furthermore, more effective quality control processes, employee and customer feedback systems, and employee reward/punishment systems should be developed in order to discourage improper restaurant employee behavior.

As the number of franchised KFC restaurant units rises, how can KFC safeguard consistent operational standards across the board, regardless of ownership? How can it ensure fairness and equality in providing ownership-blind support to all restaurants? How can it ensure full compliance from franchisees?

What are the operational implications for multi-branding in China? What operational resources and preparations are necessary in advance of any experimentation or large-scale implementation?

What are the short-term and long-term impacts on restaurant labor supply and restaurant economics from changes in population growth, labor supply, wage movements, inflation, and government legislations on workers' rights, minimum wage, family planning, social welfare, consumption incentives, waste disposal, and other aspects of environmental protection?

8. **System, Process, and Structure.** As KFC grows bigger, opportunities for things to go wrong will multiply, and the potential damage in financial and branding terms can be high. In addition to a strong crisis management system and press relationship management system, this will require continuous improvement in systems, processes, and procedures that prevent, monitor, and forewarn accidents before they happen.

Continual business growth may require changes in organizational structure. Is the Shanghai Restaurant Support Center getting top-heavy? Are the differences in characteristics of different regions and markets growing or diminishing? Should some of the resources currently embedded in the Shanghai Restaurant Support Center be re-allocated to a few regional support centers in order to better position them for future growth, develop future generations of leaders, reduce the size of a bloated organization in the Shanghai Restaurant Support Center, and more effectively serve the needs of different regional markets? Above all, how can the company keep alive the spirit of flexibility, innovation, and adaptability as KFC China grows from a teenager to young adulthood?

9. **Support From Corporate Headquarters.** As KFC China's contribution to YUM! Brands' revenue and earnings base continues to rise, the pressure for KFC China to integrate into the rest of the corporation in terms of culture, values, policies, strategies, and resources may rise over time. Going forward, KFC China can learn from KFC USA's experience of effective management of product quality through supplier management and process automation in proportion to volume and scale. Assigning senior executives from the corporate office to the China division to serve as function head or second-in-command of select functions such as human resources, QA, product R&D, and franchise management would be a good starting point.

Assigning succession candidates for leadership positions from KFC China to corporate headquarters for temporary assignments will accomplish multiple purposes including value immersion and placement under close observation.

10. **Leadership.** With help from YUM! Brands' corporate headquarters, KFC China can do an even better job with senior leadership development, especially development of local talents, and with building a company culture based on the highest standard of integrity. KFC China, in turn, can contribute even more to YUM! Brands by transferring senior local executives to YUM! Brands headquarters in the U.S. or to other strategic country markets, especially those in the developing world such as Brazil, India, Russia, and Vietnam. KFC China can also play a leading role in "exporting" East Dawning to country markets outside China, where the business potential may be far greater.

GOING FORWARD

In a large, complex, rapidly changing, increasingly pluralized market environment like China, a one-size-fits-all approach to any consumer business will lose its market relevance sooner or later. KFC is no exception. This does not mean KFC China should adopt different menus, prices, advertising, promotion, or operation standards for different regional markets in China. It may mean, however, that KFC needs

to consider changes in its objectives, values, and policies toward customers, employees, organizational structure, and resource allocation.
Specifically, these are some of the changes worth considering:

1. Revise downward the percentage growth objective for the
   China division. While there is no limit to KFC and Pizza
   Hut's growth potential in China in the foreseeable future,
   there will be a limit to the number of new KFC and Pizza
   Hut restaurants that can be opened in any fixed time period
   due to the complexity of balancing available resources over
   time, and across multiple – at times conflicting – business
   objectives.
2. Refine East Dawning, but move its market focus and resources
   to outside China. Within China, focus on KFC, Pizza Hut,
   and Pizza Hut Express.
3. Develop senior local talents within KFC China to take on
   top national, regional, and even international leadership
   roles in the next few years.
4. Strengthen employee education on basic values of quality of
   food and service, honesty, and integrity.
5. Regionalize the organizational structure. Transfer core
   responsibilities and personnel for marketing, real estate
   development, restaurant operation management, and training from Shanghai to a few regional centers.
6. Decentralize decision-making power and influence. Delegate
   more authority to regional and market offices. Gradually
   modify the culture of KFC China from top-down to bottom-
   up, inviting employee initiatives and broad-based employee
   participation.
7. Reduce the number and the frequency of new product introductions if necessary, in exchange for marked improvement
   in product quality and price performance.

CONCLUSION

According to the Chinese adage – "Tian-Shi, Di-Li, Ren-Ho" – successful conclusion of any noteworthy human endeavor requires a

good match among three elements: timing, context, and people. In the very first chapter of Sun-Tze's famous work on military strategy, he said as much. In his advice to princes and kings, Sun-Tze named five ingredients as the necessary elements in order to achieve success when waging war. First, a righteous cause under which the leader and his subjects are united; second, timing and climate; third, battlefield environment; fourth, qualities of the commander and the troops he leads into battle; and fifth, system, organization, rules, and regulations. If this does not seem familiar, take another look at Exhibit 14 of this book.

The story of KFC China is a perfect example of a good match among the people, the context, and the timing. Together, they created the necessary, but still insufficient, conditions for KFC's improbable success in China. A sound strategy backed by effective implementation filled the remaining void.

Looking ahead, as China continues with a highly dynamic process of transformation – economically, socially, and even politically – in the next few decades, only the most perceptive and swiftest-moving companies will rise to the top, and stay on top. Will KFC be able to move as swiftly in the next twenty years as it has in the first twenty? Will KFC be as flexible, innovative, and adaptable in meeting new challenges and embracing new opportunities with lightning speed as it has been in the past? Will the "Local Gang" be as good as, or even better than, the "Taiwan Gang?"

I wish I had answers to these and other questions.

Nevertheless, I am curious about how long it will take KFC to open its 10,000th restaurant in China, and whether I will be there at its grand opening. Once again, time will tell.

EPILOGUE

Born and raised in Taiwan, and educated in America, my first visit to China came in the early 1980s. I remember being nearly blinded by the air in Beijing and Shanghai, which was thick, foggy, and clogged. I later learned that the polluted air, filled with soot and other airborne particles, was due to the burning of coal used in heating and cooking throughout China.

I also recall my initial impressions of the country consisting of very few colors. At the time, only a few black cars could be seen in the streets, all of which were official government limousines of the same brand, Red Flag. The street trolleys and buses took on a slightly lighter shade of gray, wheeling alongside a massive sea of bicycles, most of which were also black. Men and women dressed alike, mostly in white shirts and dark-colored pants. Many people wore Mao suits, including most government officials. All the people I met, including company executives and factory managers, were government employees, as few private enterprises existed at that time. In addition to the dominant black, white, blue, and gray colors at every turn, green fit the dress code for soldiers of the People's Liberation Army. And red, of course, the base color of China's national flag – along with the five yellow stars – could be seen everywhere. Those were the colors. Those were the days.

In Beijing I stayed in the Beijing Hotel on Chang-An Road. This was one of the few hotels in Beijing permitted to accept foreign guests at the time. In fact, a few American companies including Boeing, Lockheed, and McDonnell Douglas, which were the first to enter China, had little choice but to set up their office inside the Beijing Hotel, while their China chief representatives would live and work out of the same hotel suite.

I had a picture taken in front of the Beijing Hotel for my mother-in-law. Her wedding had taken place there nearly half a century earlier, before she and my father-in-law retreated to Taiwan with the Nationalist Party in 1949, as did my own parents. Out of all immediate family members, both on my side and on my wife's, I was the first to visit Mainland China since 1949. As the plane approached Beijing, I couldn't control a strong sense of excitement and a strange feeling of being on the fringe of a historic mission.

One night during my stay in the Beijing Hotel, I arranged to dine with a good friend, Chen Bo Shen, in a restaurant next to the hotel lobby. He and I first met at Harvard, when I was an MBA student and Bo Shen Da Ge ("big brother" in Chinese, as he was a few years older) was studying law across the Charles River on a Chinese government grant. After receiving his LLD degree, Bo Shen Da Ge returned home to Beijing. This was going to be our first meeting in China. At 6:30 PM, we were stopped at the restaurant's entrance after being informed that the restaurant would close soon at seven. Since it was a chilly night, and culinary options throughout China were extremely limited in those days, I reminded our host that there was still time for a quick meal. Reluctantly, he seated us for dinner. Shortly after we placed our dinner order, the restaurant staff began sweeping the floor all around our dinner table. As you would expect, we quickly finished our dinner and rushed out, skipping dessert, of course. Bear in mind, this was a restaurant inside one of the best hotels in Beijing at that time. Unfortunately, like all business enterprises in China at the time, the restaurant was owned and operated by the government, without a token appreciation for service, quality, or any combination thereof. All workers were government employees, drawing the same fixed wage regardless of how busy or slow the day was, with no economic incentive whatsoever to perform, let alone outperform. Those were the days.

In Shanghai, I remember standing near the top of the Peace Hotel, overlooking the Bund. Only a few buildings in sight were taller than ten stories. The two most famous streets in Shanghai back then, as is still the case today, were Nanjing Road and Huaihai Road. The most visually striking building along Nanjing Road back in those days was the old Russian Center, which is now the Shanghai Exhibition Center. Today, it's boxed in on three sides by skyscrapers, two of which are hotels – the Portman Ritz-Carlton across the street and the JC Mandarin immediately adjacent. Along Huaihai Road, Jinjiang Hotel was one of the tallest buildings, and the best hotel available to foreign tourists at the time. Today, it is shadowed on one side by the New Jinjiang Hotel, and on the other side by the Garden Hotel.

Directly opposite the Bund on the east side of the Huangpu River is an area called Lujiazui, which is part of Pudong. Back in those days Lujiazui was nothing but marshland and rice paddies. Today, it's China's budding financial center. Tomorrow, it will vie to become "The New York of Asia" – challenging Hong Kong, Singapore, Tokyo, and Seoul combined. Ironically, today Lujiazui does resemble a mini-Manhattan from a distance.

It's hard to imagine Manhattan without the skyscrapers. Many say the same about Lujiazui. Not me. I have seen Lujiazui and Pudong going back to the days of the rice paddies, less than 20 years ago. What a difference 20 years can make, like day and night, heaven and earth.

Yet, in my opinion, none of these changes in the physical world matches in significance to the changes in the hearts, minds, and behavior of the masses. These latter changes can be witnessed in almost every facet of life, every day, on every face – from what they eat, drink, wear, read, and play to what they think and how they express themselves. Throughout the 1980s, every time I visited China I remember feeling as though I were trapped inside one of Charlie Chaplin's movies in black and white, where almost everywhere I turned, people moved about like robots with little or no expressions on their faces. People dared not open up to strangers, or even to their closest relatives, for that matter.

Today, much of that has changed. Of course, there remain sensitive political topics such as one-party dictatorship, democracy and freedom of expression, Taiwan independence, the Dalai Lama and Tibet, and Falungong, all of which many Chinese would prefer to avoid. Outside these sensitive political topics, almost all others are free for discussion, and debate. Regardless of one's view toward Chinese politics, there can be no denial that China has come a long way, even in the political arena, since the economic reforms commenced in 1978. With the economy projected to continue a path of rapid growth in the coming decades, more changes will take place in China's economic, social, and even political system, presenting enormous opportunities and challenges to those who choose to participate.

KFC's entry into China was timed perfectly. The year was 1987, a decade after the conclusion of the Cultural Revolution, but well before the beginning of the accelerated economic take-off that came after Deng Xiao-Ping's Southern Tour in 1992. Being the first foreign QSR chain to arrive in China, KFC undertook enormous political and business risks, overcame numerous barriers to entry, established first-mover's competitive advantage over its competitors, and eventually became the number-one restaurant brand in a huge and rapidly growing market. Highlights of KFC's success in China, and factors contributing to it, have been the subject of this book.

WHAT'S AHEAD FOR KFC CHINA?

At the current speed of growth, the Chinese economy can easily absorb a few hundred new KFC restaurants every year in the next few decades. In other words, in the foreseeable future, KFC China will continue to face a situation of growth constraint on the supply side of the economic equation, not on the demand side. Given KFC's current growth momentum in China and the widening gap between it and its closest competitor, McDonald's, KFC seems to be in a strong competitive position, and getting stronger. So much stronger, in fact, that I think KFC's leadership position in the Chinese restaurant industry is KFC's to lose.

During KFC's first 20 years in China between 1987 and 2007, 2,000 restaurants have been put in place. How many more will come in the next 20 years? Who knows, even if I don't see Sam Su's prediction of

10,000 KFC restaurants in China come to fruition by the year 2027, I may still be able to witness it in my own lifetime. When that happens, it will be time for an update of this book, by a future generation of leadership of KFC China.

To contact the author of this book,
please email: warrenkliu@hotmail.com

INDEX